Storytelling and QAR Strategies

Other Recently Published Teacher Ideas Press Titles

Fun with Finance: Math + Literacy = Success
Written and Illustrated by Carol Peterson

Paper Action Figures of the Imagination: Clip, Color and Create
Paula Montgomery

Fairy Tales Readers Theatre
Anthony D. Fredericks

Shakespeare Kids: Performing his Plays, Speaking his Words
Carole Cox

Family Matters: Adoption and Foster Care in Children's Literature
Ruth Lyn Meese

Solving Word Problems for Life, Grades 6–8
Melony A. Brown

Abraham Lincoln and His Era: Using the American Memory Project to Teach with Primary Sources
Bobbi Ireland

Brushing Up on Grammar: An Acts of Teaching Approach
Joyce Armstrong Carroll, EdD, HLD, and Edward E. Wilson

The Comic Book Curriculum: Using Comics to Enhance Learning and Life
James Rourke

Hello Hi-Lo: Readers Theatre Math
Jeff Sanders and Nancy I. Sanders

War Stories for Readers Theatre: World War II
Suzanne I. Barchers

Think Green, Take Action: Books and Activities for Kids
Daniel A. Kriesberg

Storytelling and QAR Strategies

Phyllis Hostmeyer and Marilyn Adele Kinsella

A Teacher Ideas Press Book

AN IMPRINT OF ABC-CLIO, LLC
Santa Barbara, California • Denver, Colorado • Oxford, England

Library of Congress Cataloging-in-Publication Data

Hostmeyer, Phyllis.
  Storytelling and QAR strategies / Phyllis Hostmeyer and Marilyn Adele Kinsella.
 "A Teacher Ideas Press Book."
 Includes bibliographical references and index.
  ISBN 978-1-59884-494-8 (pbk : alk. paper) — ISBN 978-1-59884-495-5 (ebook) 1. Storytelling—Methodology. I. Kinsella, Marilyn Adele. II. Title. III. Title: Storytelling and question-answer relationship strategies.
 LB1042.H75 2011
 372.67'7—dc22   2010036576

ISBN: 978-1-59884-494-8
EISBN: 978-1-59884-495-5

15 14 13 12 11   1 2 3 4 5

This book is also available on the World Wide Web as an eBook.
Visit www.abc-clio.com for details.

Libraries Unlimited
An Imprint of ABC-CLIO, LLC

ABC-CLIO, LLC
130 Cremona Drive, P.O. Box 1911
Santa Barbara, California 93116-1911

This book is printed on acid-free paper ∞
Manufactured in the United States of America

The authors and publisher gratefully acknowledge permission for use of the following material:

Text adapted from *QAR Now: Question Answer Relationships* by Taffy Raphael et al. Scholastic Inc./ Teaching Resources. Copyright © 2006 by Taffy Raphael et al. Reprinted by permission.

Excerpts from Raphael, T. E., & Au, K. H. (2005, November). QAR: Enhancing comprehension and test taking across grades and content areas. *The Reading Teacher*, 59 (3), 206-221. Copyright 2005 by the International Reading Association. www.reading.org

Contents

Foreword

Bundling Storytelling, QAR, and Character Education

Jim May, copyright 2009

Storytelling may be the first communicative art attempted by human beings. Once a prehistoric hunter had painted a particular act of bravery onto the wall of a cave, the proud artist would have felt a need to tell of the experience. Hoping his particular insight could serve as a contribution to his peers, the hunter would have conveyed selected details of the event. Thus both the image on the wall and the narrative endowed to the image become a part of the life of the tribe and a position of honor bestowed upon the teller as these first primordial legends were assembled.

The cave painting was then used regularly for tribal rituals. The image acted as a kind of sanctifying symbol, an icon or metaphoric reminder of an important story that remained a part of the tribe, passed forward through generations.

More stories are added during the many nights gathered around the fire experiencing the elements of heat and light that have, for centuries and up to the present, inspired humans to open their imaginations and souls to something beyond the ring of the firelight, something beyond the ordinary, something that has as its currency the attention of human imagination upon the daily acts of survival: of living, dying, and loving.

These early primordial tales became differentiated to particular landscapes, beliefs, customs, experiences, and climates. What they had in common was a core of reflecting a particular worldview, a particular set of memories that would become a certain coda that identified behaviors and practices needed for the survival of the group.

The stories of the Old and New Testament, Buddha's teachings, stories of the Hindu, the Sufi stories of Islam and the Tao, Grimm's collection of folktales, and Arabia's *One Thousand and One Nights,* to name a few esteemed traditions, all suggest the central role that narrative has played historically in the march of culture, in the seeking of truth and right action across the span of human history.

And so it is an ancient practice—and potentially a morally defining moment—when one tells a story: whether it be a teacher telling a folktale to a class, a preacher delivering a homily, or the friendly "catching up" over dinner.

About the Teller

Jim May (http://www.storytelling.org/JimMay) is a storyteller who speaks in the natural, matter-of-fact style of the fathers, horse traders, and small-town raconteurs who populated rural McHenry County, Illinois, where his family has lived since the 1840s.

For adult audiences, he tells original stories of growing up in the tiny Catholic farming community of Spring Grove. These stories that are at once hilarious and touching range from, "How to Become 'Most Valuable Altar Boy' (MVAB)," to horse trading tales and heart-warming memories of family life.

For children he offers stories from traditional sources. These folktales, myths, legends, and ghost stories from various cultures worldwide have the humor and wisdom of the great tales that have been preserved in every culture and handed down orally from one generation to the next.

Jim May's stories have taken him across the United States and Europe. He has told at schools, corporations, professional groups, and festivals across the land. Chicagoans know him from his appearances on WGN's *Roy Leonard Show* and from Studs Terkel's radio show on WFMT-FM. Jim received a 1989 Chicago Emmy award for a WTTW-Channel 11 production of his original story, "A Bell for Shorty."

In addition to telling stories, he offers workshops for professional groups and people of all ages on how to tell stories as well as how to create original stories from family heritage and personal experience.

Jim is the recipient of numerous awards including the National Storytelling Network's Circle of Excellence award for his exemplary work in his own storytelling and in bringing storytelling to others through his work as artistic director, workshops, and mentoring.

Chapter 1

Merging QAR and Storytelling

In the late 1970s, Taffy Raphael, while working as David Pearson's research assistant, began her study of classroom questioning practices. She was particularly interested in exploring the relationship among questions, the text, and the reader's background knowledge and how this relationship builds comprehension. She also wanted to develop methods for teaching the Question–Answer Relationship (QAR) effectively. Her research led to a deceptively simple method of categorizing questions: On My Own, Right There, Think and Search, and Author and Me. By using the language of QAR, teachers can help students to develop reading comprehension, to understand a wide range of concepts, and to meet the rising expectations of high-stakes testing (Raphael and Au 2005, 206).

A Sample of QAR with a Fable

On My Own

1. Have you ever tackled a job or a task that you thought would be easy, only to find that it was far more difficult than you had anticipated?

2. What did you do when you discovered that the task was too difficult for you to complete?

3. Did you seek other ways to complete the task and reach your goals?

4. Do you think it is possible to fail at a task but still learn a valuable lesson? Explain.

I am going to share a version of an Aesop fable called "A Bundle of Sticks." It is a fable about three brothers who had to fail at a seemingly simple task in order to learn a valuable lesson.

"A Bundle of Sticks," an Aesop fable as told by Phyllis Hostmeyer

An old man summoned his sons for a meeting. The oldest son, who had been working in the fields, came home immediately. The next son was playing games with friends, but he soon ended his game and also came to his father's home. And the youngest son left his studies and walked to his father's home. They found their father sitting quietly in the shade of a tree.

As they gathered around, the father turned to look at each of his sons. For a few moments, he said nothing. Then he handed a bundle of sticks bound with rope to his oldest son and said quietly, "Break this, please." The son placed his large hands around each end of the bundle and attempted to break it. He strained and strained but could not break the bundle.

The next brother laughed, grabbed the bundle away, and said, "Let me show you how to do this simple job." He also twisted and struggled with the bundle but was unable to crack even one of the sticks.

The youngest son shoved his brothers aside and said, "What weaklings. Give the bundle to me. I will succeed where the two of you have failed." Smirking at his brothers, he pried and bent the bundle with no success.

The older brothers stood back with folded arms and began to chide him, "Come on, little brother, show us *weaklings* how to break that bundle." They laughed out loud as their youngest brother's face grew red. He continued to strain until the father walked to where they stood.

The father held out his hand. "Please, hand the bundle to me, son." Accepting the bundle of sticks from his son, the father proceeded to remove the bindings. He then handed one stick to each son and said, "Break please."

Each stick easily snapped in two. The father smiled and said, "I hope that each of you has learned a valuable lesson. Unity brings strength."

Right There

1. How many sons did the father have?

2. What task did he give to them?

3. Were any of the sons successful at this task?

Think and Search

1. I am going to break the class into several small groups. I want some of the groups to make a list of the sons' behaviors and words. In other words, think back to the telling of the fable and make a list of the things the sons did and said.

2. I would like other groups of you to make a list of the father's behaviors and words. In other words, think back to the telling of the fable and make a list of the things the father did and said.

Author and Me

1. Do you think the father is a man to be admired?

2. Does the father have characteristics or qualities that you admire?

3. Why do you think the father felt he needed to teach the lesson of unity to his sons?

Why Should I Add Storytelling to My Already Full Curriculum?

The greatest teachers throughout history knew the power of storytelling. Every culture had its revered storyteller: a griot from Africa, a seanachie from the Emerald Isle, or a grandmother from Native America, who told stories to teach lessons. Somewhere along the way, perhaps with the advent of the printing press, storytelling became a pleasant diversion for children, but not much else. It was librarians who kept the tradition alive during story hours.

Then, with the renaissance of storytelling in the 1970s, storytellers stepped out of story hour and into the spotlight. Storytellers not only delighted in the pure joy of telling stories but also noticed that powerful lessons were being conveyed through story. Many storytellers, who were also teachers, began building their curriculum around storytelling. When a lesson starts with a story, a certain magic occurs. Imagination is peaked, connections are made, and the curriculum takes life.

During the telling of a story, students not only are listening with their ears, but they also see the story in the mind's eye. Storytellers use vivid images to awaken the senses of sight, taste, smell, hearing, and touch. When this happens, students visualize. Besides that, each listener becomes emotionally involved as the storyteller evokes feelings of love, anger, fear, sadness, joy, pity, and more. Listeners are taken on a roller-coaster of human emotions as they make inferences. As the listeners participate, they bring their own experiences into the story, and they make connections.

In addition, a well-told story provides clues along the way, so the listener can make predictions and draw conclusions. Listeners make comparisons, question the characters' choices and motives, and recognize cause and effect, problem and solution. Listening skills are enhanced, while increased concentration and the ability to recall information are strengthened.

The National Council of Teachers of English, in its position paper "Guideline on Teaching Storytelling," cites numerous benefits to be garnered from classroom storytelling. As children listen to stories, they learn vocabulary in context, and they absorb narrative patterns. Students then carry this vocabulary and the patterns into their own discussions and written work. Students who have enjoyed storytelling develop an awareness of audience and its role in story. That sense of audience awareness is a crucial element that enhances students' writing skills. For many students, the oral tale provides a solid path that leads to skilled composition (NCTE Guideline on Teaching Storytelling 1992).

If we have not convinced you of the power of storytelling, let us share the words from one of our favorite storytellers, Margaret Read MacDonald.

An Introduction to Storytelling by Margaret Read MacDonald

Telling stories to build character? Humans have been doing this since time began. Or at least since 2000 BC. We have cuneiform records of stories being told in Babylonia and Sumer. Those stories were full of morals. Every culture has its special stock of tales used to guide the young … and sometimes to chastise the old. Your own family likely had a few cautionary tales told to warn you away from the most dangerous or unsavory behavior.

In families, character-building tales are often trotted out in response to some bad behavior. But as teachers, we can forestall problems by sharing tales with our group *before* the problem arises. Hearing and thinking about a story, a group can build its own sense of character expectations. Shared tales can become a part of the classroom culture. Here is something you can refer to when certain situations arise.

One of my former students uses the story of Grandfather Bear in her kindergarten classroom each fall. In that tale, a chipmunk shares its winter cache of food with the hungry bear. In gratitude Grandfather Bear strokes his paw down chipmunk's back, leaving five black stripes. The class shares the story, talks about the story, acts out the story, creates art around the story, and then, during the rest of the year, whenever the teacher sees a child sharing, she simple walks up and quietly strokes her fingers down that sharing child's back—giving "five black stripes."

About the Teller

Margaret Read MacDonald (http://www.margaretreadmacdonald.com) is referred to as "a grand dame of storytelling" by *School Library Journal* for many reasons:

- Storytelling tours to Australia and New Zealand; Borneo, China, Indonesia, Hong Kong, Japan, Malaysia, Philippines, Singapore, Thailand; Brazil, Argentina, Cuba; Austria, Czech Republic, France, Germany, Hungary, Luxembourg, Poland; Republic of Georgia, Kenya, Spain, México

- Ph.D. Folklore, Indiana University; Master of Educational Communications, University of Hawaii; Master of Library Science, University of Washington

- Teaching storytelling at the University of Washington Information School and Lesley University

- Children's Librarian since 1965: San Francisco Public; Hawaii State Library Bookmobile; Singapore American School; Fairfield Methodist Girl's School, Singapore; Mountain-Valley Library System (Children's Consultant), Montgomery County, Maryland; King County Library System (1979–2002)

- Author of more than fifty-five books and audios on storytelling and folklore topics

She is the honoree of many awards including: Fulbright Scholar to Mahasarakham University, Thailand and the Talking Leaves Literary Award, established in 2001 by the National Storytelling Network to honor those who "have had a major influence and force in the literary body of storytelling."

You probably already know many of Aesop's fables. They have been used for centuries to suggest morals. But in this book, you will find many more tales that can help you shape behavior. Whether told or read aloud, sharing these stories can give your class much to consider. Read through this collection, choose a few tales that speak to you, and make them a part of your class culture.

How Will Merging QAR to Storytelling Improve Reading Comprehension?

We are living in a world of high-stakes testing. Fortunately, a plethora of research on reading comprehension instruction is also at our fingertips. Whether one is reading the work of Jeff Wormelli, Taffy Raphael, Jeffrey Wilhelm, or any one of dozens of other brilliant researchers and authors, a discussion about teaching reading strategies will surface. Various researchers will explain this range of skills and strategies in different ways and will even debate the difference between a skill and a strategy. But they will all agree that independent readers use a mixture of skills and strategies as they read.

Our students can take those same strategies and skills that help them comprehend while reading and use them to comprehend as they listen to stories. Storytelling provides all students with an opportunity to practice visualizing, making connections, inferring, and predicting. A student who lacks reading fluency spends a great deal of time and effort decoding words. This makes it difficult for that student to focus on the subtle clues an author provides about a character. Let's return to the fable "A Bundle of Sticks." The student who reads the fable and is struggling to decode the words may not notice that the youngest son pushes his brothers aside. This one gesture implies a great deal about the relationship among the three brothers. A struggling reader may not notice that the father speaks quietly or looks in silence at each of his sons before asking them to break the bundle of sticks. Again, visualizing the father's body language and actions gives the reader insight to the character.

In contrast, the student who listens and watches as a storyteller tells the fable can focus on the gestures and words of each character. The storyteller can provide clues about a character through body language, voice, and facial expressions. Students can then draw conclusions about the relationship of the three brothers and why the father felt that it was crucial to teach the lesson of unity. They can make inferences about the father's character traits. As they listen, students begin to make predictions and ask questions, "Will they be able to break the sticks? Why does the father need these sticks broken? I'll bet the father knows a trick, and he will break the sticks at the end." Students who have developed the ability to make inferences and predictions with an oral story will have at hand many of the strategies needed for comprehension when they pick up a text and read.

QAR serves as a framework to ensure that the necessary strategies are introduced and practiced. By using QAR, students learn which type of question can be answered before reading, during reading, or after reading. They learn how to find and use information as they construct answers. Students also learn how to merge the information found in a text with their own background knowledge (Raphael and Au 2005, 213). The types of questions developed for reading comprehension are the same types of questions that can be used for storytelling. It is our intention in this book to provide librarians and teachers with interesting character education stories supported by questions in each of the QAR categories.

Listening versus Reading

Differences exist between reading a story and hearing a story. Readers and listeners engage with a story differently. First, let's look at what a reader does. The reader uses the structures of text—headings, paragraph breaks, and illustrations—to build comprehension. A reader also monitors comprehension by controlling the pace and can choose to skim a section or return to a passage and reread. In addition, readers must use a range of skills and strategies, such as visualization and making an inference, to catch the subtle clues an author provides.

A student listening to a story builds comprehension differently. The listener builds comprehension by relying on the storyteller's voice, body language, and facial expressions. Listeners cannot control the pace of a story. Instead, it is controlled by the teller, who might send images rapid-fire and later use pauses to give the listener time to absorb images. Unlike the reader, the listener has no option to return to a story to skim and scan; therefore, a teacher as teller may need to retell stories or lead a guided discussion as students develop their listening skills.

Students using a text to answer questions develop and use the necessary skills of scanning, note-taking, summarizing, making connections, among others. While students listen to a storyteller, they use many of those same skills. Students who have heard a story cannot physically return to a text and scan it, but they develop the ability to listen and to scan the memory. They are able to discuss and dialogue with other students. Reading and listening are symbiotic. As students develop listening skills, reading comprehension is also enhanced through the development of skills and strategies.

In 1991, the United States Department of Labor identified listening as one of three basic foundation skills necessary for success in the workplace (Secretary's Commission on Achieving Necessary Skills [SCANS] 1991, 3). In addition, the Standards for Language Arts require that "Students develop an understanding of and respect for diversity in language use, patterns, and dialects across cultures, ethnic groups, geographic regions, and social roles" (NCTE 1996, 3). Storytelling provides the perfect avenue for developing that understanding and respect.

QAR Categories Explained

QAR is far more than a framework for reading comprehension. It empowers students. Once students can determine the type of question being asked, they know where to go for the answer. This became evident to Phyllis many years ago in her classroom: "Before they learned QAR, my students often read a question, threw down their pencils, and wailed, 'This is a stupid question. The answer isn't in the book.' The students were partially correct. The answer wasn't in the book, but that did not mean the question was stupid. Unfortunately, as a novice teacher, I did not understand the categories of questions and sometimes ended up agreeing with my students. In my very best teacher voice, I often said, 'There seems to be a problem with question number three. The answer isn't in the book. Let's just skip that question, boys and girls, and answer the other ones.' Oh my, what a difference QAR made in my classroom. Once my students and I understood the type of questions, we eliminated the *stupid question* label."

Taffy Raphael and her colleagues explain that questions, depending on the source of the answer, fall into two main categories: *In the Book* and *In the Head*. *In the Book* questions are exactly what their name implies. Students answer questions by using information found in the book or text. The text might be a newspaper article, a text book, a chapter book, or an advertisement. For our purposes, students will be using information from the oral story to answer QAR questions. *In the Head* questions require students to tap into their background knowledge and, in some cases, merge that knowledge with material from the text. Let's take a closer look at the four types of questions (Raphael and Au 2005, 212).

Right There

When students are dealing with a Right There question, they can find the answer in the text they have read or in the story they have heard. If using a text to answer questions, students can scan the text and put a finger directly on the answer because it is located Right There (Raphael, Highfield, and Au 2006, 23). With storytelling, the student has actually heard the answer spoken. No inferences are required. The answers are usually short, and sometimes words from the question might also be found in the answer. For example, after telling the fable "A Bundle of Sticks," we can ask a Right There question such as, "How many sons did the father have?" The answer, "He had three sons." The answer was stated Right There at the beginning of the fable.

The Right There question-and-answer relationship does not change whether using a text or an oral telling. What changes are the skills the student must use to find the answer. A student using a text to answer a Right There question can be taught to skim and scan or to refer to notes. The student who is answering questions after an oral storytelling must rely on listening skills, memory, and discussion.

Think and Search

Think and Search questions can also be answered by locating information in the text, but students must look several places in the text or possibly look at several texts (Raphael, Highfield, and Au 2006, 23). When answering a Think and Search question following an oral telling, students must think through the entire story and recall a range of details. They need to remember what they visualized, what they heard, and what they saw the teller doing. This means that the teacher as teller might need to tell the story more than once. To support students while they tackle the Think and Search questions and activities found in this book, we have included a range of activities and graphic organizers. Graphic organizers can help the students to map the details and determine a hierarchy of importance. We have also included visualization activities and reenactments that will help students to recall the sequence of events.

We have found that one of the most powerful aspects of Think and Search questions is their relationship to the Author and Me question. When we first began using QAR, we thought we had covered all the bases if we had at least one question in each of the four categories. We could not understand, then, why students often put little effort into answering the Think and Search question, or why they still gave little more than empty stares when asked an Author and Me question. Why wasn't QAR working in the classroom? It was not working because often we had structured Think and Search questions to be nothing more than busy work. Let's look again at "A Bundle of Sticks" to understand this.

Following the telling of "A Bundle of Sticks," we chose to give students a Think and Search task to complete. Working in small groups, students discuss the story and make a list of the characters' actions and words. Some groups make a list of the brothers' behaviors, others of the father's behaviors. Once these lists are completed, the students use the information to make inferences about character traits, motivation, and feelings. In other words, students use the information that they gathered in Think and Search to answer the Author and Me question.

Once we understood this relationship between Author and Me and Think and Search, it changed the way we wrote questions. Because the Author and Me question requires the most complex inferences and synthesis of information, we write those questions first. We then backtrack to create questions in the other three categories. Those questions provide concrete information that students can use to make the inferences and draw conclusions needed when answering an Author and Me question. The Think and Search questions are no longer busy work. They now provide a base of information that can be used to make the inferences and conclusions used to answer an Author and Me question.

Author and Me

Author and Me questions require that students use comprehension strategies that link text-based information with the student's schema, or background information (Raphael, Highfield, and Au 2006, 26). This is the skill required on the extended response portion of many state and nationally normed tests. We have found that students find these to be the most difficult of the QARs to answer. But Author and Me questions become manageable once students understand the relationship between Author and Me and Think and Search. Once again, let's look at "A Bundle of Sticks" to understand this relationship.

If the first question the students encounter after hearing the fable is an Author and Me question, the students must grapple for abstract information. For example, let's imagine that the first question posed to students after the telling is, "Does the father in 'A Bundle of Sticks' have any character traits that you admire?" Many students are still trying to process the sequence of the fable. They are still dealing with any visualizations that they have formed during the telling. They may have focused so closely on the actions of the sons that they aren't even aware of the subtle actions of the father. Asking them about character traits before they have had a chance to look more closely at a character's words and actions requires that they try to explain an abstract concept without providing an opportunity to process their thoughts. It is cognitive overload.

If the students first make a list of the father's behaviors and words, they are working with a more concrete task. They can recall the words of the teller and create a list—a physical object. They can list the following actions of the father: the father stared at his sons before speaking to them; he spoke quietly; he asked them to *please* break the bundle; he waited in the background while the sons struggled with the bundle. Students can now use the information garnered in the Think and Search to draw conclusions and make inferences required by the Author and Me. They can infer that the father was patient because he waited in the background while each son struggled with the bundle. They can draw the conclusion that he was a loving father by the way he looked at each son in silence before giving the task. Perhaps they will visualize him sitting under the tree prior to calling his sons and infer that he was contemplating death and worrying about how his sons would survive without him.

We have had students who think that an Author and Me question is an opinion and therefore feel that any answer is correct. This is a misconception that needs to be addressed. Students need to understand that good opinions are based on accurate information. For example, let's imagine that we have posed the Author and Me question, "Why do you think the father felt a need to teach the lesson of unity to his sons?" If a student responds with the idea that the father is probably a fault-finder who constantly preaches and yells at his sons, we would have to ask, "What in the fable supports your answer?" If there is nothing in the fable to support the student's belief that the father is a fault-finder, then the answer is not valid. Students need to see that their opinions should be based on concrete information found during the Think and Search. If they create a list of the father's actions and words, they can make a valid inference about his character traits.

On My Own

On My Own questions are closely related to the Author and Me questions. Often we pose these questions to students before a reading or a storytelling event. These questions help to activate prior knowledge and provide subtle clues about the story they are about to hear (Raphael, Highfield, and Au 2006, 26). Before telling "A Bundle of Sticks," we have students begin to think about and discuss times that they tackled a task that turned out to be more difficult than they first imagined. Or we might choose to ask them if they think people can learn a valuable lesson from failing at a task. On My Own questions can be answered by all students in the classroom, to varying degrees. They tap into their schema or background knowledge to find answers. On My Own questions often help students to make a connection to the characters. For example, students may have said that when they found the task to be too difficult, they just gave up. Others might say that they turned to someone else for advice or help. Some might say that they tried to hide their failure so that no one would know they failed. Their personal experiences with a similar situation can help students to connect to the characters in the fable.

Another interesting characteristic of On My Own questions is that they often have a dual-purpose. For example, before telling "A Bundle of Sticks," we might ask students if they had ever learned anything valuable from failing at a task. After telling the fable, we might return to that On My Own question for further discussion. Following the discussion of the value of failing, we can ask, "Do you think the brothers learned anything from failing to break the bundle?" We might have asked an On My Own question such as, "What types of things do people do that show they respect someone? What types of things do people do that show a lack of respect?" After hearing the fable, we can return to that On My Own question and ask students whether they now have any new ideas concerning how we show respect or lack of respect for others. Did the fable provide any new ideas? Perhaps in the discussion before telling the fable, they did not mention that laughing at someone is disrespectful. They can now add that idea to the list because it happened in the fable. The author or storyteller has provided material that encourages thought, but the student is drawing the final answer from their own schema.

In This Book

We have gathered eighteen "stories" from some of the best storytellers we know. The book contains fables, historical pieces, folktales, and myths from a range of cultures. The stories have been divided into grade levels, with one chapter for Grades 3 and 4, one for Grades 5 and 6, and a final chapter for Grades 7 and 8. We have included a fairy tale, African American fables, a legend from Senegal, wisdom tales, historical pieces, and autobiographical pieces. Readers will also find Jewish folktales as well as a folktale from the Marshall Islands. We have included tales from Japan, China, and India, as well as Greek and Native American myths. For every story, we have created QARs and activities related to QAR. Most of the stories have several questions in each of the QAR categories, especially in Author and Me. We have purposely done this so that teachers can select the questions that will best fit the needs of their students. It is not necessary nor effective to pose all of the Author and Me questions presented in our book. Choose the questions that best meet your goals and the needs of your students. We have also provided On My Own questions to be used before and after the telling. Answers to the QARs were intentionally not provided to promote student discussion. The important part is to encourage dialogue to help each student reach an individual definition of the character education traits.

Chapter 2

How to Tell a Story

We hope we have convinced you of the power of story in the classroom. We have provided eighteen stories tied to the character traits of caring, citizenship, fairness, honesty, respect, and responsibility. Yes, you could just read these to the students. You could give them a copy of the story to refer to as they work to answer questions. But you will be robbing yourself of one of the great joys of teaching if you do not *tell* the stories. You will be robbing your students of those magical moments when they hear a story and time is suspended. Become a teller of stories. We promise the inherent power of story will capture your heart—and those of your listeners.

We recommend that you, as a novice storyteller, choose a short folktale or fable as your first telling piece. Fables and folktales have great characters, a moral tucked inside, and a story line that has lasted for hundreds, even thousands of years. Once you have told a few of these, you are ready to tackle all of the stories in this book. You are ready to build your repertoire of stories.

Ten Steps to Becoming a Teller

1. Find a story that strikes a chord. Does it tickle your funny bone? Does it support your value system or echo your sentiments? Does this story please your sense of aesthetics? Sometimes it isn't until months after the first reading that tellers discover why a certain story has appeal. They just know that it is a story that must be told. Tellers listen to their inner voice as it guides them to stories they love. At first, some of the stories that we offer in this book may not strike that chord with you. That is why we have offered Telling Tips after each story. These are suggestions that the teacher as teller can use to make adjustments and develop an ownership of the stories.

2. Memorize your prayers, your songs, your pledges, and your lines for plays, but not your stories. Read the story all the way through several times. Learn the sequence and the plot structure, but do not memorize it.

3. Now that you have completed several readings, put the text away, and don't look at it until you are ready to tell it in your own words. To do this, start by sequencing the story in your mind. To make this easier, we have provided a Story Map for each story. Visualize each scene like pictures with lots of detail. Always review this sequence, especially when first telling a story. We call this process "reducing the story to its bare bones or the story map." Try one of the following activities to create a mental map of the story.

    a. Fold a paper into eighths and draw one scene in each square. Use this the first few times you practice telling. Then put the paper away and visualize the pictures as you practice your next tell.

    b. Walk your way through the story and associate a hand movement or gesture to help you transition through the major parts of a story. For example, if you are telling the story "Little Red Riding Hood," you might put your hand aside your mouth—a visual clue that mother is calling to Red. Your next gesture might be a pointed finger, which serves as a reminder that in this section, you will relate mother's warnings about staying on the path and not talking to strangers. Many people are kinesthetic learners and find it easier to remember the sequence of gestures. These become hooks that trigger the next part of the story.

    c. John Walsh, the president of International Learning Solutions, also discourages tellers from memorizing a story. He suggests that tellers try to place a story in a room of their home. No matter where the teller is working, the visual of the room carries him or her through the story. The door might be the introduction, an easy chair is the next important event, a window is the next important event. Each event is mentally tied to a spot in a room (Walsh 2003, 23–29).

    d. Write each main scene on a different colored note card. Place them in order. As you tell the story, you can connect each scene with a different color to help you transition from one scene to the next.

4. Next, make the story your own. Do this by reading different versions of the same story (the Internet is a good place to track down new versions). Think about the characters in the story to determine their personalities and character traits. Create compelling dialogue and play with the words. Look for lines or gestures that repeat, and use those for audience participation. Let the gestures, facial expressions, pauses, asides, and emotions be natural to you.

5. Practice a strong beginning and ending. Know exactly how you want to begin the story so that you can grab your audience immediately. Know exactly how you want to end so that the closing is crisp and clean. The rest of the story can be semi-rehearsed to keep the lines fresh. This allows the teller to add nuances, asides, and new interpretations while remaining true to the tale.

6. Write down your version or at least the bones of the story once it is a "keeper." Don't be too quick to put pen to paper, because once the story is written, you will be less apt to play with it and improvise.

7. TELL IT!! Tell your story to the walls, your kids, the dog, a mirror or even while you are in the car with the radio turned off. Grab every opportunity you can to tell the story to people.

8. Talk to your audience before you begin. Let them know who you are or little bit about why you are telling the story. Ask some On My Own questions. It is good to get your audience thinking before you start, but keep it short. We have supplied some ideas for On My Own questions with each story in the book. Select the questions that best suit your final goals.

9. Now, trust yourself to let the story take wing. Your flight won't always be on a charted course, but that's okay. In fact, go ahead and make mistakes. Sometimes tellers stumble onto the best part of a story through mistakes. Keep in mind, your audience will have no idea that a mistake was made . . . unless you tell them. Students are a storyteller's best audience. Not only do they enjoy, but they dynamically respond to stories,

10. The best critique of the story? The faces of those listening. Give your story some time to settle in and to find the right audience. New stories are like a new pair of shoes; they may be shiny and new, but sometimes they pinch a little. With time you will slip into the story with comfort and ease.

The great thing about this process is that you will never forget the story. Once you have told a story and have used *your* words, *your* images, *your* nonverbal communication skills, and *your* emotional context rather than those of someone else, the story becomes a part of you.

Steps Three and Four Revisited

Parts three and four are the crux of the ten steps. The following is an example of how to learn the story path and to add one's own words to the much-loved Aesop's fable called "The Boy Who Cried Wolf." First, there is a translated version written long ago. Then there are the processes used to learn it, and, finally, the story as a storyteller might tell it.

Aesop's Version

A shepherd-boy, who watched a flock of sheep near a village, brought out the villagers three or four times by crying out, "Wolf! Wolf!" and when his neighbors came to help him, he laughed at them for their pains.

The Wolf, however, did truly come at last. The shepherd-boy, now really alarmed, shouted in an agony of terror: "Pray, do come and help me; the Wolf is killing the sheep"; but no one paid any heed to his cries, nor rendered any assistance. The Wolf, having no cause of fear, at his leisure lacerated or destroyed the whole flock.

There is no believing a liar, even when he speaks the truth.

The Learning Process

After visualizing the story, choose a method that suits your style of learning. These first two methods presented in this section are similar. It is not important to draw well. Stick figures will suffice.

Story Map Method: On a piece of paper draw a picture of the shepherd calling out "Wolf!" Draw an arrow to the next picture of several people running. Draw an arrow to the next picture of the boy laughing and the villagers' angry faces. Draw an arrow to the words "Repeat two times." Draw an arrow to a picture of a wolf and the scared face of the boy.

Draw an arrow to the boy calling for help. Draw an arrow to the wolf eating the sheep. Draw an arrow to the words "There is no believing a liar, even when he speaks the truth."

Folded Paper Method: Fold a plain paper into eighths. Number each square. Box 1—draw the shepherd and some sheep. Box 2—boy calling out "Wolf!" Box 3—villagers running to his rescue. Box 4—Boy's face laughing. Box 5—villagers' angry faces. Box 6—terrifying wolf face and scared boy face. Box 7—boy calling "Wolf!" and Wolf carrying off sheep. Box 8—Write out the moral of the story. For many people, the numbers provide a stronger memory hook than a series of arrows. This same method can be done using eight note cards, each one a different color.

Outlining or Sentencing Method: Use full sentences or phrases rather than pictures.

1. Shepherd cries "Wolf" for help twice and villagers respond.

2. Boy laughs at villagers.

3. The wolf comes.

4. The boy is terrified and again calls for help.

5. No one comes.

6. Wolf eats sheep.

7. Moral: *There is no believing a liar, even when he speaks the truth.*

Tape the Bones Method: Auditory learners may prefer to listen to the bones of the story until they have committed just the bones to memory.

Walking the Story Method: Kinesthetic learners often use the sentence outline and mime the story. Exaggerate every movement. It provides the body with muscle memory that helps one to remember the story map.

Making It Your Own

Now that you know the story map, you are ready to make it your own. Some tellers rely on creative dramatics and allow the story to unfold in the moment of telling. Others like to play with words, and they craft the story first. Most tellers do a combination. As you read the following version, notice the choices the teller made. Details, images, and dialogue have been added to the fable.

Once, long ago, there was a young boy who tended a flock of sheep atop a tall hill that led to the village. All day long, the boy sat and watched the sheep. Sometimes he became so bored with no one to talk to, except the sheep. He longed for some excitement, but what could he do? He had to tend the sheep. Then, one day, he had an idea. He took his bullhorn and blew into it with a mighty wind. [sound of horn.] The sound echoed throughout the valley below. That was the signal for the village folk that the shepherd boy was in trouble. They dropped what they were doing and ran up the hill. As they got closer, they could hear his voice calling out, "Wolf, Wolf, a wolf is trying to get the sheep!" The people scrambled to the top of the hill looking for the wolf.

Huffing and puffing, they sputtered, "Where is it? Where is the wolf?" There was no wolf anywhere!

There was no wolf, only the boy laughing at his own joke. "You should have seen your faces," he laughed, "all red and puffy. You look so funny!" The people did not laugh. Their faces turned from concern to anger.

As they turned around to go, one of the men said harshly, "You betrayed our trust. We counted on you to be true to your job. You should never call for help when none is needed. This is not funny!"

A few days later, the boy was once again bored. He remembered how the townspeople looked as they huffed their way up the hill, looking for the wolf. It would be even funnier to see it a second time. So, again he took his bullhorn and let the sound alarm the village below [sound of horn]. When the people heard the alarm, they thought surely the lad would not try such a trick again. So they took their weapons and trudged up the tall hill. But, again when they got there, they were greeted by the boy sitting in the tree laughing at them. This time the man, who had talked to the boy before, did not say a word. As he looked at the boy, the man's eyes said it all . . . you have disappointed your community, your friends, and, most of all, yourself.

Now, the boy realized that his tricks were not funny. He vowed never to do it again. However, just a few days later, a wolf did come. The boy was so scared, he took his bullhorn and blew the alarm. When the townspeople heard it, they just shook their heads "Fool us once, shame on you; fool us twice, shame on us . . . you will not fool us three times," and they went back to work.

All day long, the boy sat hugging the limb of the tree as the wolf scattered the sheep. The boy felt helpless and sorry for his flock. At the end of the day, the villagers wondered why the shepherd boy did not return. When they went to find out, they found the boy sitting in the tree crying. "Why, why didn't you come, when I called?!" he cried.

As the man helped him out of the tree, he said, "Trust is a funny thing. It takes years to prove you are trustworthy, but only one lie to break it down. Now, come with us to find your sheep. Show the people that you are willing to pay for your lack in judgment, and slowly you will once again enjoy the trust others will have in you."

Decisions

The main thing to remember as you learn a story is to have a sense of play. This is not work—it's fun! As you tell the story over and over, you will begin to find out what works and what does not. You will develop your own style. Here are some choices that you can make:

- Will you sit or stand as you tell?

- Will you use gesture and movement, or let the words tell the story?

- How will you pace the story? Where will you slow it down or quicken the pace?

- Will you add participation, props, or musical instruments?

- Where will you pause for effect?

- Will you use asides to the audience, or keep to the narrative?

- How much emotion will you add to your voice and face?

Good speech techniques will also make you a better teller:

- Look at the audience. Actually look into the eyes of an audience member and say a word or a phrase directed toward that person. Avoid sweeping back and forth with your eyes, making no real eye contact.

- Enunciate your words.

- Modulate your voice—pitch, volume, and tempo.

- If you are standing, avoid pacing and rocking or any unnecessary movement. It is a distraction.

Sometimes new storytellers find that bringing a story down to its bare bones is daunting. In Chapters Four through Six, we provide the stories and have reduced each one to the bare bones with a Story Map. By doing that step for you, we hope to make learning the story easier and bring you one step closer to being a "Teacher as Teller."

Chapter 3

Activities Tied to QAR and Character Education

Definitions of the Character Traits

To match stories to character traits, we have created our own definitions for *caring, citizenship, fairness, honesty, respect,* and *responsibility.* Definitions for these character traits abound in packaged programs, Internet sites, and classrooms. Please feel free to reword our definitions to match the goals of your character education program.

Caring

Caring people are kind and willing to lend a hand to those in need. They are also willing to forgive those who have hurt them. Offering a sincere thank you is a trademark of people who care. Synonyms for caring are *thoughtfulness, consideration, kindness, compassion, generosity,* and *helpfulness.* "Too often we underestimate the power of a touch, a smile, a kind word, a listening ear, an honest compliment, or the smallest act of caring, all of which have the potential to turn a life around" (Leo Buscaglia, 1925–1998, author, motivational speaker, and professor at University of Southern California, http://www.quotationspage.com/quotes/Leo_Buscaglia).

Citizenship

People can show good citizenship in many ways. People who are good citizens help to make their community a better place to live. They donate time and money to community projects. They show respect for authority by obeying the laws and the government of their community. They are thoughtful of their neighbors, the environment, and all public places. Good citizens vote in elections and respectfully voice their opinion on issues. Synonyms for citizenship are *nationality, patriotism,* and *allegiance.* "Never doubt that a small group of thoughtful, committed citizens can change the world. Indeed, it is the only thing that ever has" (Margaret Mead, 1901–1978, American cultural anthropologist, http://www.quotationspage.com/quotes/Margaret_Mead).

Fairness

People who are fair try to listen to others and keep an open mind. Fair people follow rules and do not try to take advantage of people who are having troubles. They do not try to profit from the misfortune of others. A fair person will take turns and share with others. Synonyms for fairness are *tolerance, justice, evenhandedness,* and *impartiality.* "Fairness is what justice really is" (Potter Stewart, 1915–1985, associate justice of the United States Supreme Court, http://www.brainyquote.com/quotes/quotes/p/potterstew114112.html).

Honesty

Honesty means telling the truth no matter how difficult it might be to do so. An honest person is straightforward. Synonyms for honesty are *sincerity, truthfulness, integrity, frankness, candor,* and *openness.* "Honesty is the first chapter in the book of wisdom" (Thomas Jefferson, 1743–1826, third president of the United States, http://www.quotationspage.com/quote/36707.html).

Respect

One way people show respect is by using good manners. Respectful people don't use curse words or improper language. Respectful people do not hurt other people, or even threaten to do harm. Those who practice respect strive to solve arguments peacefully. Respectful people accept the fact that others might think or behave differently. Respectful people think about other people's feelings and try never to hurt their feelings. Respectful people have respect for themselves, and then treat others the way they would like to be treated. Synonyms for respect are *esteem, reverence, value,* and *admiration.* "Self-respect permeates every aspect of your life" (Joe Clark, 1938–, former principal of Eastside High School in Paterson, New Jersey, http://www.quotationspage.com/quote/3318.html).

Responsibility

Responsible people pause and think about the consequences of their actions. A responsible person might ask, "If I do this, will others be hurt? If I do this, what will happen as a result of my actions? If I do this, will it make my community a better place?" Responsible people don't push off work onto other people; they use their talents to make the world a happier place. Responsible people don't give a halfhearted effort and then make excuses for failure. They strive to do the best they can and keep on trying even when things become difficult. Synonyms for responsibility are *dependability, reliability,* and *conscientiousness.* "We have to do the best we can. This is our sacred human responsibility" (Albert Einstein, 1879–1955, theoretical physicist, http://www.alberteinsteinsite.com/quotes/einsteinquotes.html).

Theory Behind the Activities

According to the theoretical framework of Lev Vygotsky, social interaction is necessary for full cognitive development. If we want our students to understand the concepts of character education, we must provide opportunities for social interaction. An understanding of concept happens at a social level before it happens at an individual level (Vygotsky 1978, 57). Students will internalize personal definitions of caring, citizenship, fairness, honesty, respect, and responsibility only after we have provided ample opportunity for them to examine these concepts with their peers.

When students are given opportunities for social interaction, they will develop an understanding of concepts far beyond any understanding that they could develop individually. Vygotsky referred to this potential for cognitive growth as the "zone of proximal development." Because they are helping one another and receiving adult guidance, students in the zone of proximal development will reach goals and have the ability to do things that they would never have accomplished while working alone.

In his excellent book *Action Strategies for Deepening Comprehension*, Jeffrey Wilhelm provides seven reasons for using enactment strategies in the classroom. Obviously, enactments tap into the social aspect of learning posited by Vygotsky. However, Wilhelm also cites that enactments can be used in all stages of reading—before, during, after—and enactments are highly motivating. Enactments encourage students to think and visualize. But perhaps the most powerful aspect of enactments is their ability to provide a transformative experience for students. Enactments offer a path for students to consider their views of the world, to develop a sense of self, and to form ethical standards (Wilhelm 2002, 9–15).

Smorgasbord of Activities

The activities that we present throughout our book can be used with almost any story that has been included. However, we have assigned certain activities to each story. We considered our own success stories and our own classroom experiences as we paired activities with stories. For example, we have found students in grades 3 and 4 to be most receptive to Freeze Frames, whereas students in the upper grades seem to be more comfortable with activities such as the Walk and Gawk that provide them with opportunities to discuss concepts and work in social groups.

The following sections provide step-by-step directions for each activity and a sample of a completed activity. To create the samples, we have used the fable "A Bundle of Sticks." Obviously, no one would actually do all of these activities with one fable. We simply used that fable repeatedly because we are all familiar with it, thereby making it easier to understand the activity.

The activities are listed in alphabetical order to make it easier to locate them. Directions for the activities will not be provided in Chapters Four through Six; however, samples and suggestions can be found where appropriate. Please refer back to this chapter for full directions and samples of each activity.

Anticipation Guide

An anticipation guide should be presented to students before the telling of the story as an On My Own activity. The guide will have statements that are related to the story. Students read the statements individually and then decide whether they agree or disagree. After they have heard the story and completed the QARs, students can return to the anticipation guide as an Author and Me activity.

Often they find that their opinions or ideas have changed as a result of the ideas presented in the story and the post-discussion. Encourage the students to share the ideas in the story that helped them to form their final opinion.

Anticipation Guide for "A Bundle of Sticks"

Before	Statement	After
	It is always easier to get a job finished if you have a friend to help you.	
	Sometimes failing at something is a good way to learn something new.	
	One of the best ways to learn something new is to sit and listen to an older person give an explanation.	
	We should be polite even to people who are rude.	
	We don't need to say "please" and "thank you" when we are with our family.	

Freeze Frame

One of our favorite enactment activities is Freeze Frame. As storytellers and educators, we have been using Freeze Frames successfully with students for many years. Although this activity can be used at any grade level, we have chosen it to be the predominant activity for the stories in grades 3 and 4. Wilhelm offers a similar activity with several variations; he calls it Tableau (Wilhelm 2002, 125–130).

Directions for Freeze Frame

1. Students will work in teams of three to five.

2. Provide each group with a scene from the story that they have just heard. Write each scene on a separate 3 × 5 card; one card for each group. The group is given no more than ten minutes to interpret the scene and decide how they will present it. (Whenever we are suggesting Freeze Frames for a story, we have also suggested scenes for the enactment.)

3. Explain to students that creating a Freeze Frame is an Author and Me activity because they must determine the feelings and emotions of the characters. What facial expressions and posture will they use to convey those emotions to the audience?

4. Once each team has had an opportunity to practice the Freeze Frame, have them return to their seats. The team that has the first scene comes to the front of the room. The remaining students should close their eyes and place their heads down while the team sets up their Freeze Frame.

5. When the Freeze Frame is in place, instruct students to raise their heads, observe the Freeze Frame, and decide which scene they are seeing.

6. Lead a discussion of the Freeze Frame. The goal is not simply to determine the time and place of the scene. Rather, students need to go deeper and determine what each character is feeling at this point. Read the body language and facial expressions. Read the position of the characters. How do you know what each character is feeling and thinking? What has helped you to make that inference? By merging their background knowledge with the telling of the story, students can make inferences and draw conclusions—clearly an Author and Me activity.

7. Repeat this process for each of the groups.

Freeze Frame with "A Bundle of Sticks"

To do Freeze Frame with the fable "A Bundle of Sticks," the first step would be to select the frames. Here are five possible scenes:

1. Father thinking while sitting under a tree.

2. Father preparing to hand the bundle of sticks to sons.

3. Youngest son grabbing the bundle from his brothers.

4. Brothers chiding the youngest son.

5. Father sharing the lesson of unity with sons.

Because five scenes have been selected, five teams of students will be needed to create the Freeze Frames. You will also need five note cards, one per scene. Give a card to each team and allow team members no more than ten minutes to determine how they will stage their Freeze Frame. Scene 1 contains only one character, the father. So how will a team of five students be involved in the Freeze Frame? Some students can play the role of the tree; others might take on the role of the son who is working at a distance in the field. The idea is for the students to visualize what is happening and determine how they will use body language to represent that scene.

Consider the team working to create scene 4, the brothers chiding the youngest son. Three students could play the role of the brothers and one the role of the father. Remind them that these scenes are frozen. They cannot actually laugh out loud or move around as they chide the brother. The student enacting the role of the youngest brother cannot move as he demonstrates attempting to break the sticks. They cannot change position once the class has been invited to see the frame. Also, they must decide where the father will be during this scene and what his body language will convey.

Once students have correctly identified the scene, lead a discussion about the feelings that are being implied in the Freeze Frame. What did the students do to convey the feelings? What body language or facial expressions were employed? Do the students agree that the feelings being conveyed at this point are accurate? For example, the students presenting the Freeze Frame may have decided to enact the father as angry. The students observing the Frame might feel that is inaccurate. Why?

Graphic Organizers

Graphic organizers are thinking tools. They provide students with a visual of abstract concepts and show the relationships among ideas. A strong graphic organizer can be used to keep students focused during discussions and dialogue. By entering ideas and information into graphic organizers, students create a storehouse of information that can be used as they create final products.

Throughout this book, we provide a variety of graphic organizers. An understanding of the QAR categories makes it easier for students to complete an organizer. Many of the graphic organizers presented in this book can be used before, during, and after the telling of the stories. Let's look at how some of these graphic organizers are related to QAR.

Graphic Organizers and QAR

Many students tend to do fine while filling out the first two columns of the graphic organizer that follows. They can list ideas from the story that help to answer the question, and they can often give one sentence to explain their thinking. But students need ample opportunities to share their thinking. They need to learn how to share what they are visualizing and inferring. Their connections and observations need to be explained in depth and the third column demonstrates ways to do that.

Question or Prompt		
Story Says	**I Think**	**Help Others to See and Understand Your Ideas**
Once students understand the question or prompt, they must return to the story to garner ideas. This is a Right There/Think and Search activity because students are listing things that they have heard in the telling. They do not need to make an inference at this point.	Now students look at the ideas they have listed and explain the connection between what they have listed and the question being asked. This is an Author and Me activity because they are explaining the relationship between their thoughts and the words of the story.	This column is also Author and Me work. By discussing symbols, word choice, and body language that was used in the story, students can help others to understand their ideas. Use any of these techniques to help others understand your ideas: • compare and contrast • analyze word choice, symbols, or literary devices • make connections • visualize • infer and imply • draw a conclusion • explain gestures or facial expressions used by the teller

Sample of Graphic Organizer for "A Bundle of Sticks"

Question: Was the Father a Man to Be Admired?		
Story Says	**I Think**	**Help Others to See and Understand Your Ideas**
Father sat under tree thinking, then he called his sons.	The father gave some serious thought to the best way to teach his sons a lesson.	I think the father was really worried about all the fighting going on among his sons. Sometimes when I have a problem, I just do anything to make it go away. I don't always think about the consequences, and then I end up making the problem worse.
Father always says please and speaks quietly.	Even though the sons are rude, the father still says please.	I admire people who talk courteously, even though everybody around them is being rude. The father will not give up his values just because his sons are rude. He always uses his good manners.
The father speaks quietly and waits while the sons try to break the bundle.	He doesn't resort to yelling at his sons; he stays calm and quiet.	I think if I were the father, I would have been yelling at the boys because they seem to fight all the time. But he just stays patient and waits for them to fail. If he would have yelled, the fighting would have just been worse.

I Am Poem

The *I Am* poem (adapted from Yopp and Yopp 2006) is a format that has been popular in classrooms for many years. The idea of the *I Am* poem is to have students come to an understanding of a character's thought process, feelings, concerns, and character traits. This activity can be used with any of the stories in the book, but we have chosen to pair it most often with stories in fifth grade or higher. (For another lesson plan that uses the *I Am* format differently from our use, see Ideas Plus, Book 20, 2002, 21–23.)

Directions for *I Am*

1. You will need a stack of note cards in two colors. Select from the following prompts, I hear, I see, I touch, I say, I want, I dream, I hope, I pretend, I feel, I wonder, I worry, I cry, I understand, I try, I decide, I taste, I believe, I doubt, I fear, and write one prompt per card. We usually select fourteen prompts from the list, but the activity works as well with fewer prompts. The prompts selected from the list will all be on the same color note card.

2. Next, using four note cards of a different color, write the following phrase on each card: I am . . .

3. Divide students into manageable groups of five or six and give a set of note cards to each team: four cards with the words "I am" and ten to fifteen cards with the prompts listed above. Each team must select a character from the story they have heard. For example, if a team decides to be the father in "A Bundle of Sticks," they will take the four note cards that say "I am" and write "the father" on each card. They will take the remaining cards and complete each sentence as though they are the father speaking.

4. Explain to students that the cards can be completed with Right There information or Author and Me information. For example, if they write, "I see my sons trying to break the bundle of sticks" they are using information that is Right There in the fable. But if they choose to write, "I see problems looming for my sons," they are providing an inference or insight into the father's thoughts. It was never said that the father sees trouble looming; they must infer that idea. This is Author and Me.

5. Once the students have completed all of the cards, they now arrange all of the cards in any order that they feel creates the most powerful poem. Many students choose to open and close the poem with an "I am" card and use the two remaining "I am" cards to open or close more stanzas. The order of the cards and placement of ideas leads to interesting discussions among the groups.

Sample of *I Am* Poem Using "A Bundle of Sticks"

Notice in the two sample poems that the lines have been arranged differently. By placing each line on a separate card, the students can manipulate the lines of the poem to create an arrangement that best conveys the message they have garnered from the story.

Have students read the final poems and juxtapose two characters from the same story. It provides students an opportunity to discuss the differences of opinions that two characters might have. Another interesting option is to have the students put their poems in the same order and then take turns reading lines. For example, the father would read his line that begins "I see," followed by the son reading his "I see" line. The father would then read his line that begins "I touch," and the son would read his line that says, "I touch." They could then read their respective "I am" lines at the same time. Reading the poems in this style creates a dramatic and powerful presentation that helps students to recognize the differences and similarities in opinions and beliefs.

I am the father.	**I am** the oldest son.
I wonder how much longer I will live.	**I wonder** why my father has called us together.
I pretend that I do not hear my sons squabble every day.	**I pretend** not to be irritated by my brother playing games and reading all day.
I understand that there are lessons that must still be learned.	**I dream** of working the land unlike my foolish brothers.
I want to help my sons.	**I am** the oldest son.
I am the father.	**I am** the oldest son.
I am the father.	**I touch** the bundle of twigs my father hands to me.
I see my sons approaching from three directions.	**I want** to break the bundle and show my strength.
I touch each boy's face before I speak.	**I try** and try and try to break the sticks.
I dream of the men they will become.	**I worry** that I look weak and foolish in front of my brothers.
I try to give them a simple task to complete.	
I worry that they will fail.	**I am** the oldest son.
I am the father.	**I cry** tears of laughter as my brothers also fail.
I cry unseen tears when my sons shove one another.	**I hear** the name-calling from them.
I hear name-calling and laughter that ridicules.	**I feel** relieved that they cannot break the bundle either.
I feel an ache in my heart, my soul.	**I see** my father untie the bundle.
I hope my sons have learned.	**I hope** that I have not disappointed my father.
	I understand the lesson that he is trying to teach.
I say unity brings strength.	**I say**, yes, unity brings strength.

Metaphors and Similes

To help students understand an abstract concept, we need to help them visualize it. By comparing an abstract concept such as honesty to something concrete, students can develop a deeper understanding of the abstract. A metaphor simply allows students to visualize or express an idea adeptly. Metaphors and similes are so ubiquitous in our language that often we do not even realize we are speaking metaphorically. "The explanation was crystal clear." "We made a whirlwind trip over the weekend." "He painted himself into a corner." Each of these is a metaphor.

In his book *Metaphors & Analogies: Power Tools for Teaching Any Subject*, Rick Wormelli says, "There is nothing in the K–12 curriculum that is so symbolic or abstract that we could not create a physical comparison that would sharpen students' understanding" (Wormelli 2009, 61). It may sound like a bold claim, but it is one with which we strongly agree. That doesn't mean that every metaphor will be a good metaphor, but the benefit is in the creation of and discussion about the metaphor. So let's create some metaphors.

Directions for Creating Metaphors

1. The best time to create metaphors for the character traits is after students have had ample opportunity to discuss them. Once they have begun to develop their personal definition of honesty or citizenship, it is time to begin constructing metaphors and similes.

2. Create a set of note cards that compare one of the character traits to a concrete object. Be sure to select concrete objects that are relevant to the students. Suggestions are provided:

   a. Caring is a cell phone.

   b. Citizenship is a bridge.

   c. Fairness is a football.

   d Honesty is an MP3 player.

   e. Respect is an interstate highway.

   f. Responsibility is a microwave.

3. Place students in small teams, and give each team a note card. Challenge the team members to extend the metaphor until they have created a short free verse poem.

4. Once the metaphors are completed, have students share. Question the metaphors. Wormelli suggests that this is the time to "play the devil's advocate." Does the metaphor work, or can it cause misconceptions? Does the metaphor do anything to provide new insights? Is the metaphor flawed? How can we improve this metaphor? (Wormelli 2009, 25–26).

Metaphors for "A Bundle of Sticks"

Concepts addressed in "A Bundle of Sticks": unity, patience, courtesy

Initial Brainstorming

Patience is a rap song.

It has roots that go back many years.

It provides rhythm to our daily lives.

People sit up and take notice when they hear it.

Some people are good at it, and others aren't.

Some people know how to be patient, and others don't.

Different cultures show patience differently.

It can make a bad day better.

Everyone can be patient.

You need to practice patience.

Using the brainstorming, revise and create a free verse poem by adding, deleting, rearranging, or changing lines:

> *Patience is a rap song.*
> *It has changed with times.*
> *It changes from place to place.*
> *But we have no doubt*
> *It gives the days a rhythm.*
> *It gives a face a smile.*
> *So practice patience every day.*

Sample of an extended metaphor for Unity:

Unity is a patchwork quilt.
One little scrap might not look like much.
But sew each scrap together with cunning and skill.
Then soak up the warmth and comfort it brings.
Unity is a patchwork quilt.

Predictions about Characters

Students in your classrooms will have a range of prior knowledge. Some might have a great deal of prior knowledge about a topic, whereas others have limited knowledge. The more we can help students to activate prior knowledge, and the more we can help students to build knowledge, the more we can help them to comprehend at a deeper level. This activity will tap into the prior knowledge that students have about characters, people, and situations.

Making predictions about characters works best in stories that have three or more characters. In storytelling, we try to limit the number of characters included in a story so that the story is easier to follow. Introducing a menagerie of characters in storytelling can easily confuse the listeners. If you have a story that you think might be difficult for the students to follow, this prediction activity can help them by introducing the characters prior to the telling.

Directions for Predictions about Characters

1. Explain to the students that they will be meeting a certain number of characters, and then provide names or occupations.

2. Now tell the students that you are going to give them words or phrases that can describe the three characters they will be meeting in the story.

3. Read the first word; have students repeat the word.

4. Ask if anyone can explain the word or provide a definition. Allow a student to define the term; you will provide additional information as needed.

5. Following each explanation, ask students to connect the word or phrase to one of the three characters; make a prediction. For example, which character do you think will be honest? Why did you select that character? Are you basing your prediction on someone you know or someone you have read about in a different story? Have students explain their choices. It is perfectly all right to assign a word to more than one character. This is an On My Own activity because the students have not yet been introduced to the story. They must use their own schema to make predictions that connect the words to characters.

Example of Making Predictions about Characters with "A Bundle of Sticks"

In this story, we will be meeting four characters: a father and his three sons. Let's predict which character will have the following traits or characteristics:

Characters in the Fable

| Father | Oldest Son | Middle Son | Youngest Son |

Characteristics and Traits:

| Old | Impatient | A Student | Likes to play games |
| Rude | Patient | Respectful | Worried |

Students would now assign the words to the characters and explain their reasoning. After hearing the story, return to the chart and reassign words. Some words can be reassigned because of Right There information. It says Right There in the fable that the father is old. It says Right There that the youngest son is a student. But the text never uses words such as *patient, impatient,* and *rude.* So the students must draw that conclusion based on the actions and words of the characters—Author and Me work.

Story Impressions

In story impressions the teacher supplies students with a list of words that will appear in a story. The students read the list to make sure they know what all of the words mean. They then work in teams to create a story that uses all of the words in order (Johns and Lenski 1997, 255).

We have adapted story impressions to be used with storytelling. Rather than provide students with a list of words prior to the telling, we suggest providing them with a list of key words after the telling. Students can then work in small groups and use the list as they try to re-create the story. This retelling reinforces concepts, structure, and plotline. When story impressions are completed before having heard a story, it is wise to limit the number of words to keep the task of creating a story manageable. When the students have already heard the story, and the goal is for the students to recreate it, a larger number of words can be provided. This bank of words will help students to recall the plotline and retell the story with accuracy.

Directions for Story Impressions

1. Tell the story to the students.

2. Give students the list of words.

3. Students work in small groups to retell the story.

4. Complete the QARs.

Story Impressions for "A Bundle of Sticks"

Old man → meeting → sons → fields → games → school → bundle

oldest son → grabbed → weaklings → laughed → father

untied → break → unity

Verb Poems

This is a simple activity that we have used in our classrooms for years and years to teach nouns and verbs. Again, it helps students bring concrete structure to an abstract concept. Students can write these poems before hearing a story then return to them to make revisions after they have heard the story.

Directions for Verb Poems

1. Select a person who can be seen using the character trait being studied. Note: the students will not be writing about a character in a story. They are writing about an occupation or a person who exemplifies a character trait or a lesson to be learned from the story.

2. Use that person's name or title as line 1 of the Verb Poem.

3. Subsequent lines of the poem are verbs and verb phrases that demonstrate how that person practices the character trait. Each line of the poem begins with a vivid verb, and the closing line reiterates the character trait.

Sample of Verb Poem about Unity, a Concept Presented in "A Bundle of Sticks"

Our basketball team
Stands in a huddle
Encourages all players
Looks for the open player
Passes the ball with precision
Gains position for the rebound
Runs the plays from practice
Cheers from the bench
Holds the trophy high over our heads
Unity makes us a winning team.

Walk and Gawk

Walk and Gawk, which is also known as a carousel walk, provides students with a chance to learn in a social setting. This activity provides kinesthetic learners with a chance to move during the learning process as well. Walk and Gawk can be used before students hear the story to tap into students' On My Own knowledge. By returning to the material after the telling, students can think about the words and ideas of the story to add additional ideas, which is an Author and Me activity. We have paired this activity with all of the stories used for grades 7 and 8.

Directions for Walk and Gawk

1. Post seven large sheets of chart paper around the room. Write one of the following questions at the top of each piece of chart paper.

   a. What are synonyms for (character trait)?

   b. What is (character trait) connected to? Or, where might we see (character trait)?

   c. Why is (character trait) important?

   d. What does (character trait) never look like/sound like?

   e. What does (character trait) look like/sound like?

   f. How can (character trait) be encouraged?

   g. What can discourage (character trait)?

2. Discuss each of the questions with the students to make sure they have an understanding of what is being asked. Brainstorm one answer for each question, and write it on the chart paper.

3. Create seven groups of students, and assign each group to stand by one of the chart papers. Give each group some time to discuss its question and brainstorm additional answers.

4. Give students a signal to move to the next piece of chart paper. Give the group time to read the work of previous students and discuss additional answers. Classroom management tip: Give each group a different color marker which they will carry with them from chart to chart. This makes it easier to track the work of each group and determine when the groups have exhausted ideas. It is not necessary for the groups to work with each chart. When you see that the groups are not contributing new ideas, have them return to their seats.

5. Lead a class discussion with each chart.

6. Tell the story and answer the QARs.

7. Let students return to the charts and add additional ideas that have come about after having heard and discussed the story.

8. The final step is to have each student write an essay, poem, narrative, or personal definition of the character trait using the information on the charts. This is a perfect opportunity for students to take an abstract concept such as caring, citizenship, or honesty and demonstrate what it actually looks like, sounds like, or feels like when put into practice.

Sample of Walk and Gawk with "A Bundle of Sticks"

The idea is to make an abstract concept more concrete for students. Samples of possible answers for each question are provided. Many of the answers will be provided before hearing the fable. Once students have heard the fable, they can add to these ideas. Before letting the groups work on a chart, lead a discussion and model the activity by writing one answer on each chart. Be sure to return to the charts after a discussion of the story.

1. What are synonyms for unity? Oneness, harmony, agreement

2. What is unity connected to? Sports teams, families, national pride

3. Why is unity important? People can help each other, can provide support in times of need, can make people feel safe if they are part of a united group

4. What does unity never look like/sound like? Preventing people from joining a group, fighting,

5. What does unity look like/sound like? People working toward a common goal, teams working together to win a game, everyone standing to show respect for the flag

6. How can unity be encouraged? Thanking people for their help, giving praise to people for doing a good job

7. What can discourage unity? Blaming other people for your mistakes, calling someone names

Sample Expository Essay Based on Information Garnered during Walk and Gawk

Notice the concrete examples of unity in the following essay. The essay clearly shows what unity sounds like, looks like, and feels like. Show students how concrete ideas and examples from the chart papers can be embedded into an essay. Giving students a chance to brainstorm ideas before writing provides them with specific ideas and examples that can be used as support statements in their compositions.

Harmony, agreement, teamwork—any of these words can be used as synonyms for unity. I had never given much thought to the importance of unity, but I now realize that unity makes me a stronger, happier person.

As an American I have many opportunities to show a united front. When I am dressed in my basketball uniform and our team stands at attention during the national anthem, I am part of a united group. It makes me feel proud to hear the notes of our anthem soaring through the gym and to know that I am one with Americans all over the world. I have that same feeling of pride every time I go to a parade and stand at attention when the American flag comes by. I am always amazed to see the change in behavior when the red, white, and blue of our flag approaches. One minute everyone is laughing and cheering, shouting at friends, and scrambling for candy thrown from floats. And the very next second, the parade route becomes a united front of proud Americans standing in silence and saluting our flag.

Not only do I see the power of unity as an American, I also understand how the idea of unity makes my classroom a better place to learn. When we work in peer groups, I love to be with my best friends. Recently, I had to work in a group with students that I did not know very well. I didn't think I would like being in that group. But because everyone in the group had a chance to talk and share ideas, I learned a lot. I did like working with this united group because it made learning a lot easier. Another time I was part of a group that had to work on a presentation. One of the students in our group was a great artist. Another student knew how to use Photoshop on the computer. When each of us shared our special talents, we created a final presentation that earned us all an A. We got that great grade because we worked as a united group. I would never have done that well working by myself.

I can't do much with only one piece of a puzzle. But if I have all of the puzzle pieces, I can unite those pieces and make a really great picture. Life is just like that. Whenever I play and work as part of a united group, I can end up with a great life.

Why Did You Do It Poem

Allowing students to recode information helps them to transfer information and access it at a later date. Recoding, in its simplest form, means changing information and ideas from one form into another. For example, students hear a story about citizenship. If they then take the ideas from that story and write a poem, they have recoded the story. Recoding requires that the students make inferences and interpret what they have heard (Sprenger 2005, 67).

The *Why Did You Do It* poem provides students with an opportunity to think about a character's motivation and character traits. This is an Author and Me activity because it requires that students merge information from the text with their own ideas.

Directions for Why Did You Do It

1. Write the following questions on note cards. Create one note card for each of the questions, but make four note cards that ask "Why did you do it?"

   - Why did you do it?

   - What was the weather like?

   - Would you do it again?

   - Was anyone else there?

   - Were any strangers present?

   - Do you have any regrets?

   - Were there any distinct sounds?

   - Were there any distinct smells or odors?

   - Were you successful?

2. Shuffle the cards and place them face down in front of the students.

3. As each student draws a card, he or she answers it as a character from the story. Continue to draw cards until all are answered.

4. Once students have answered the questions, they begin to manipulate the answers and move them around to create a poem that flows. Students revise and construct the poem by adding, deleting, changing, and rearranging the cards. They might decide to rewrite a response to a question.

Example of Why Did You Do It for "A Bundle of Sticks"

Question	Father's Response
Why did you do it?	I did it because I felt the days of my life growing shorter.
What was the weather like?	The sun cast gentle rays through the boughs of an old tree.
Were any strangers present?	I looked at my sons and wondered, "Where are the sweet boys I raised? Who are these rude young men?"
Why did you do it?	I did it to squelch the worries that plagued my days.
Were there any sounds?	The cracking of three small twigs ended the rude laughter and insults.
Were you successful?	I can only hope a lesson was learned.
Why did you do it?	I did it because I am an old man in the winter of life.

A Final Activity

One of the goals of telling and working with the stories is for each student to develop a personal definition of caring, citizenship, fairness, honesty, respect, and responsibility. However, we also think it is important that students recognize that these traits should be practiced by all people, not just students. To broaden their understanding of the traits and to help them realize the importance of practicing the traits, we offer one final activity.

Character Traits across the Generations

What does respect look like to a preschooler? What does respect look like to a student your age? What does respect look like to an adult? What does respect look like to a senior citizen? Encourage the students to write one sentence that answers each question. The sentences should contain a vivid image that clearly shows the character trait enacted at each age level. (For a different lesson plan that uses the idea of abstract concepts across the generations see *Ideas Plus,* Book Four, p. 15.)

Sample Sentences for Character Traits across the Generations

Respect by a preschooler: When my grandpa comes to our house to visit, I always help him carry his suitcase to the bedroom.

Respect by a student: I never take anything from another student's desk unless I have first asked permission to borrow.

Respect by an adult: After the picnic, I canvassed the area to make sure that we had not left plastic bags or paper plates littering the grass or the beach.

Respect by a senior citizen: The workers at the fast-food restaurant are fifty years younger than I, but I always give them a smile and say please and thank you.

Responsibility by a preschooler: Before I go to bed, I pick up all of the Lego Blocks scattered about the room.

Responsibility by a student: I make sure to complete my homework before I plop down in front of the television for my favorite show.

Responsibility by an adult: I would love to buy a new MP3 player, but first I have to pay the mortgage, the utilities, and insurance.

Responsibility by a senior citizen: To make sure I understand all of the new laws, I took a senior citizen driving class offered at our city hall.

One Final Note about Activities

Remember, most of these activities can be used with any of the stories presented. Use your expertise to select from the smorgasbord of activities presented here. We have paired activities to each story based on our own work in the classrooms. Enjoy!

Chapter 4

Stories, QARs, and Activities for Grades 3 and 4

See Chapter 3 for instructions and samples of all activities.

Caring

Pre-Telling—On My Own

What does it mean to care for someone? To help others; to lend a hand? What are some things you could say to friends to encourage them to be caring and helpful, rather than uncaring? Once a basic definition of caring is established, brainstorm with the children to complete the chart below. The goal is to make the abstract concept of caring for something or someone concrete. Help the students to visualize specific situations and what it could look like and sound like when they show that they care. Suggestions for answers are provided. Help them to see that sometimes it may be difficult to be caring if all those around you are acting differently. Or there may be times that it takes a long time to help someone, and you feel impatient. It is only natural to feel put out or inconvenienced, but the mature person rises above that to choose what is right.

Caring for Someone: To Help Others; To Lend a Hand; To Be Considerate and Thoughtful	
What might caring look like?	Picking up something that someone drops; holding a door; helping to carry things; going to get help for someone who is hurt or who has fallen on the playground; sharing with others
What might caring sound like?	May I help you? You're welcome. Do you need help? Are you okay? I can help you. Let me find someone to help you.
How might caring make you feel?	Proud of myself; happy to know I helped someone; worried that others might laugh at me, if I help someone they don't like; impatient because it might take a long time to help someone; upset if the person I cared for doesn't say thank you; happy when I see that I have done something good for others

"The Queen Bee," a Grimm Brothers' tale, as told by Jane Stenson

Once upon a time there lived a man with three sons. The two oldest sons were spendthrifts and n'er-do-wells. They cared only about themselves. They frittered away their time and squandered their money. The youngest son was hardworking, caring, and cheerful.

One day the two older boys came to their father and said, "Father, we are going out into the world to seek our fortune." Their father wished them well and off they went.

The father and his youngest son enjoyed their time at home working together and helping each other. But after a time, the youngest son said to his father that he, too, wished to go out into the world, find his brothers, and seek his fortune. The father held his son close for a few minutes, then gave his blessing, and sent him off into the world.

Soon the young son met up with his brothers, who said, "What are you doing here?"

The youngest brother replied, "I've come to join you to make my way in the world and find a fortune." Laughing and laughing, the older brothers said, "We who are older haven't found our fortune yet; what makes you think you can find yours?"

"Nevertheless," said the youngest, "I would like to try." So they all walked on together.

Soon, they came to an anthill. For a bit, they watched the ants scrambling in and out of the hill, carrying food and building tunnels. "Say," said the oldest brother, "let's scruff up these anthills and kill all the ants!"

"No," said the youngest. "The ants have done us no harm; leave them alone."

"You are so boring," said the oldest brother who walked away and left the ants to their work.

The three walked on, and soon they came to a lake where many mother ducks were swimming with young ducklings in tow. "Oh, look at that!" said the older boys as they licked their lips. "Let's shoot the fattest of those ducks and roast them for our dinner."

"No!" said the youngest. "They have done us no harm. The forest has plenty of other food for our dinner. Besides, those are mother ducks, and we must leave them alone."

"Here we go again," said the older boys as they rolled their eyes.

As they continued through the forest, they spotted a tree with honey oozing down the side and a large beehive in its boughs. "Ah!" said the older brothers. "Let's build a fire at the base of the tree and smoke out those bees. It will be fun to make them go mad!"

"No!" said the youngest brother. "The bees have done us no harm; leave them alone."

"That's enough!" said the older brothers. "Are you going to continue on this journey with us, or do you want to go home? You never like any of our ideas." The younger brother did not answer but walked on with his brothers.

After a while they came to a large manor surrounded by fields. The manor was completely made out of stone. Everything on the property was also made of stone: the grass, the trees, the fields, the sheep, even the cows. There was nothing that was not stone!

The brothers walked to the front door and knocked. When no one answered, they eased the door open and walked in. Everything on the inside was also made of stone: the drapes, the tables, the chairs, the light fixtures, the rugs, even the cookies on the plate. There was nothing that was not stone!

They walked through every part of the manor until they came to a closed door at the back of the house. They knocked lightly then opened the door. As they peeked inside the room, they found an old man seated at a table. He looked up and asked, "What brings you to my home?"

The brothers replied, "We have come to seek our fortune."

"Well," said the old man, "you may have come to the right place. For you see, I used to be a king. Many years ago an evil enchantress cast a spell on my manor and everything was turned to stone . . . everything, except for me and my three daughters. To break the spell, we need someone brave enough, strong enough, and smart enough to accomplish three tasks between sunup and sundown. The one who succeeds will inherit half of my property and the right to marry one of my daughters. But be warned, those who fail any task will be turned to stone."

"Half of a kingdom! The right to marry a princess! Oh, I would surely like to try!" said the oldest brother.

The next morning at sunup, the oldest brother was given the first task: to find one thousand pearls that had been scattered about the castle grounds. The brother searched all day. He scoured the barns, looked inside every pot and kettle in the kitchen, searched under chairs and beds, but by sundown he had found only two hundred pearls. He was instantly turned to stone.

On the next day, the middle brother searched the grounds, but he found only five hundred pearls. He was also turned to stone.

On the third morning, the youngest brother sat on the steps of the manor. He put his head in his hands and a tear slid down his cheek. The queen of the ants approached him and asked, "Why are you crying, my friend?"

"Because I have to find a thousand pearls by sundown, or I will be turned to stone like my two older brothers. I don't see how I can accomplish the task and break the spell."

The queen of the ants replied, "Several days ago you saved the lives of my colony, so now we will save yours." The queen called to her colony and soon had all the ants scouring the grounds of the manor and gathering pearls. They brought them to the youngest brother who gave them to the king. The king thanked him and said, "You best get a good night's rest; tomorrow's task will be even more difficult."

The next morning, the king met the boy on the bank of the lake. He explained, "The enchantress who cast this evil spell threw my king's ring into the lake. Today you must find my ring by sundown, or you will be turned to stone."

As the young boy stood staring at the lake, the queen of the ducks swam to him and said, "Hello, my friend. You look troubled; can I help you?"

He explained the problem, and the duck replied, "You saved the lives of my sisters and our ducklings, so now let us save yours." The ducks repeatedly dove to the bottom of the lake . . . and dove to the bottom of the lake . . . and dove to the bottom of the lake. Just as the sun began to set, one duck rose to the surface with the ring in her bill. She gave it to the youngest son, who gave it to the king, who put it on his finger. He smiled at the young man as he clasped his hands close to his heart. "Thank you, my son; tomorrow brings your final task."

As the sun rose the next day, the youngest son approached the king's room for the third and final task. "Stop! Stop there at the door," said the king who sat at the table with his three daughters. "On the lips of one of my daughters is a drop of syrup. On the lips of another is a drop of sugar water. And one daughter has a drop of honey on her lips. You may not approach them, but must stand in the doorway and choose the princess who has a drop of honey on her lips. Accomplish this task, and you will inherit half of my kingdom and may marry one of my daughters. However, if you fail, you will be turned into stone for all eternity."

The young man stared at each princess but had no idea which one had the honey on her lips. Just then the queen bee flew through an open window, circled the young man's head, and then alighted on the lips of one princess. Smiling, the youngest son identified her as the princess with honey on her lips, and the spell was broken!

Everything returned to its natural form: the sheep, the grass, the trees, the chairs and tables, even the cookies on the plate. His brothers also came alive.

In due course, the youngest brother married the princess with the sweet honey on her lips. They say that they ruled the kingdom with kindness and compassion for all . . . even for the tiniest of creatures. And they all lived happily ever after.

About the Teller

Jane Stenson is an award-winning teacher and storyteller. A classroom teacher for more than forty years, she currently teaches kindergarten at the Baker Demonstration School in Wilmette, Illinois. The school is affiliated with National-Louis University, where Jane is an adjunct professor. Jane coauthored *Literacy Development in the Storytelling Classroom* (Libraries Unlimited 2009) and *The Storytelling Classroom: Applications across the Curriculum* (Libraries Unlimited 2006).

Telling Tips

The dialogue in this story is important, but putting it into your own words will make this tale easier to tell. Sometimes you might choose to say the words as the narrator without using the voice of the character. Too much dialogue can be confusing, but a slight change in voices or mannerisms will help students to keep characters straight. You need to find the right combination of dialogue and narrative for your comfort.

Story Path

Like many fairy tales, this one relies on the magic of three. Remembering each set of three will help you to visualize and bring a smooth flow to the story.

1. Three sons—two leave to find their fortune; soon the third follows.

2. Three times, the young son stops the older brothers from causing harm: he saves the ants, the ducks, and then the bees.

3. The brothers arrive at the manor to find the king and three daughters.

4. The brothers are given three tasks: to find the pearls (the two oldest brothers fail and are turned to stone), to find the ring in the lake, and to determine which daughter has the drop of honey on her lips.

5. Three animals return to help the youngest son with the tasks: the ants find the pearls, the ducks find the ring in the lake, the queen bee finds the drop of honey.

6. The son and a princess marry and rule happily.

Right There

1. How many sons are in this story?

2. Why are the sons leaving home?

3. What had happened to the manor that the brothers found in the forest?

4. Who is living in this manor?

Think and Search

1. Describe how the brothers responded to their younger brother every time he stopped them from hurting the animals.

2. List the three animals that the older brothers wanted to hurt.

3. List the three tasks that needed to be completed to break the spell.

4. Create a story map that sequences the main events of the plot.

Author and Me

1. How do you think the younger brother felt every time his older brothers laughed at him or rolled their eyes at his ideas?

2. Why do you think the younger brother continued to stand up to his brothers and stop them from doing bad things?

3. What might have given the younger brother the strength to always stand up to his older brothers and stop them from doing bad things?

4. How do you think the older brothers acted toward their younger brother once the evil spell was removed and life was restored to them and everything in the manor?

5. Now that you have heard the story, let's return to one of our On My Own questions. Has the author helped you to think of some things you might say to one of your friends to encourage them to be caring rather than uncaring?

Post-Telling

Return to the graphic organizer that was used pre-telling. Has the story helped the students think of other ideas of what it looks like or sounds like to show they care? Also, how might it make someone feel to know that others care? Add these new ideas to the graphic organizer.

Freeze Frames

1. The youngest brother meets up with his two older brothers, who laugh at him when he says he wants to find his fortune.

2. The older brothers ask the younger brother if he wants to go home since he doesn't like any of their ideas for having fun.

3. The brothers ease open the door of the manor and walk in.

4. The oldest brother asks for a chance to try the three tasks.

5. The youngest brother stands in the doorway wondering which princess has the honey on her lips.

6. Everything in the castle is released from the evil spell and returns to life.

Additional Sources

Books

Fox, Mem. *Wilfrid Gordon McDonald Partridge.* Brooklyn, NY: Kane/Miller Book Publishers, 1989.
    Mem Fox has created a beautiful story about a caring relationship between a young boy named Wilfrid and Miss Nancy, who lives in a retirement home next door. Unfortunately, Miss Nancy loses her memory, but Wilfrid takes on the task of helping her find it.

Mundy, Michaelene. *One Caring Kid: A Book about You—And What Your Kindness Can Do!* Charlotte, NC: Elf-Help Books for Kids, 1999.

Sierra, Judy. *The Beautiful Butterfly.* Boston: Houghton Mifflin Harcourt, 2000.
    In this Spanish folktale, a butterfly turns down several suitors before meeting a gentle mouse. She chooses him because his sweet song will lull their babies to sleep. Mouse falls into a pond and is swallowed by a fish. A chain of events follows in an attempt to end the cries of the grieving butterfly.

Web Sites

http://www.crayola.com/lesson-plans/detail/caring-concentration-lesson-plan
    This Web site has lesson plans and activities on caring from the Crayola Company.

Citizenship

Pre-Telling—On My Own

What are some definitions of the word trouble? How many ways can we use the word *trouble* in a sentence? Here are a few suggestions:

• Don't trouble me; I'm busy.

- I am having trouble with these math problems.

- Can I trouble you to bring me another cup of coffee?

- That bully that lives down the street is nothing but trouble.

- My arthritis is giving me a lot of trouble today.

- The blue ribbon that I won makes it worth all the trouble I put into my picture.

- We got into trouble with the teacher when we started yelling in the hallways.

Think about a time that you or someone you know was in trouble. Maybe you didn't do your homework or finish your chores at home.

Think about something that someone might do that could cause a lot of trouble—playing with matches, telling a lie.

Think about things that might cause some trouble for you—a poisonous snake, a bully, a broken shoestring, a flat tire.

In this story, pay attention to the word *trouble*. Monkey is making trouble trying to figure out what trouble is until he is face to face with real trouble.

Story: "Monkey Finds Trouble," an African American fable from the Caribbean, as told by Lyn Ford

Monkey was sitting near a little house. From inside the house came sweet aromas that made Monkey feel hungry. Monkey peeked in the window. A woman was making cakes. One cake was cooling on the kitchen counter. One cake was baking in the oven. One cake was still batter in a bowl, batter that smelled good.

Monkey saw the woman pouring things into the bowl and mixing and stirring the batter for another cake. As she added ingredients to the bowl, the woman spoke to herself, "Here is good brown sugar. It makes the batter sweet. Yum! And here is spicy cinnamon. It makes the cake good to eat. Yum!"

Monkey saw the woman pick up a bottle. She pulled a cork from the bottle, pop! Then she shook the bottle over the bowl. The woman shook the bottle harder and harder until something brown oozed from the bottle—glug, glug, glug. But the bottle slipped from her hands and fell to the floor. The bottle broke—*CRASH!* And all the sweet, sticky molasses became a puddle on the floor.

"Oh, look at this!" shouted the woman. "All this trouble on my floor! Now I'll have to go into town and buy more!"

The woman took off her apron and hung it over a chair. Then she put on her hat. Then she reached into her apron pocket, removed some money from it, and put the money into the pocket of her skirt. The woman walked out of the house and down the road to town.

Monkey climbed through the window. He tiptoed over to the puddle on the floor. Monkey said to himself, "Well, now, that woman said this stuff is Trouble. I have never tasted Trouble." Monkey stuck his long fingers into the molasses; he licked his fingers and smacked his lips.

"Mmmm," said Monkey. "Trouble is a sticky situation! But Trouble tastes good! Trouble is sweet! I think I'll go into town and buy some Trouble, too!"

Monkey didn't have any money of his own, but he had seen where the woman kept her money. He reached into the woman's apron pocket and took some money. Then Monkey walked out of the house and down the road to town.

Monkey saw the woman leaving a shop. She carried a bag as she walked toward her house. Monkey walked into the shop. He saw a man standing behind a counter. Monkey saw cans and jars on shelves; he smelled fresh fruit and vegetables. Monkey saw lots of foods, but monkey wanted only one thing. Monkey walked up to the man behind the counter and said, "Take this money and give me Trouble."

The shopkeeper said, "Excuse me. Did you say you wanted trouble?"

"Yes," said Monkey. "Bring me lots of Trouble."

"Monkey, do you know what trouble is?" asked the shopkeeper.

Monkey thought about the sticky, sweet molasses he had tasted on the woman's floor. "Yes," he said, "I know what Trouble is. Trouble is good. Trouble is sweet. I love Trouble. And I've given you money. Bring me lots of Trouble!"

The shopkeeper scratched his head. Then he went into his backyard. He came back with a big bag that was tied shut. The bag wiggled and squirmed and made panting and whimpering sounds.

"Here, Monkey," said the shopkeeper as he handed the top of the bag to Monkey. "When you open this bag, I am sure you will find trouble."

Monkey dragged the bag far out of town. He didn't want to share his Trouble with anybody. As the bag bumped and thumped down the road, whatever was inside it made whimpering and growling sounds.

"Oh, this Trouble is nice and fresh!" laughed Monkey.

When he was alone in the tall grass, far away from everybody, Monkey opened up the bag. Out jumped the shopkeeper's dog! The dog chased Monkey, and barked and barked, "Rowf! Rowf! Growf!"

Monkey ran and ran and finally climbed a tree. Monkey stayed in the tree. He cried, "Oh, why, oh, why did I ask for Trouble?"

When the dog grew tired of barking at Monkey, it went back to the shopkeeper in town. But Monkey stayed in that tree for a long time. After that, Monkey knew more about trouble. He knew: Trouble is not good. Trouble is not sweet. And nobody should go looking for trouble.

About the Teller

Lyn Ford is an award-winning fourth-generation Afrilachian storyteller, a former preschool teacher, and an Ohio teaching artist with the Greater Columbus Arts Council and the State-Based Collaborative Initiative of the Kennedy Center (OSBCI). Lyn is also a Thurber House mentor for young-author writing sessions and camps and a contributing author for two teachers' resources on storytelling and literacy, *The Storytelling Classroom* and *Literacy Development in the Storytelling Classroom* (both published by Libraries Unlimited). Lyn's work has been recorded on CD and included in story anthologies and magazine articles. Visit her Web site at http://www.lynfordstoryteller.com or send her an e-mail at friedtales@aol.com.

Telling Tips

This folktale is fun to tell. You can exaggerate the words and make funny "monkey faces." You can also add sound effects that your audience can repeat after you. It would also be an excellent story to do some creative dramatics or even as a narrative play. The structure is fairly simple with only three scenes in the story. Introduction: 1. The kitchen. 2. The store 3. Outside in the tree. The storyteller repeats a line twice: "Trouble is good, trouble is sweet." Then the third time she says it, it changes. Trouble is *not* good. Trouble is *not* sweet. And *nobody* should go looking for trouble. Doing that emphasizes the moral of the story in a fun, non-didactic way. But to make the lesson clear, you might try saying the final line slowly and emphasizing each word.

Story Path

1. A woman is baking cakes and spills the bottle of molasses on the floor.

2. Monkey overhears the woman declare, "All this trouble on my floor."

3. She leaves to go buy more molasses.

4. He wonders what trouble is, so he goes into the house and tastes it. Not understanding that "trouble" has more than one meaning, he steals some money from her apron and goes into town.

5. He watches her go into a store to buy something.

6. He goes in after she leaves and says to the grocer, "I came to get some trouble."

7. The grocer misunderstands Monkey, thinking he is going to do harm. So he puts a big dog in a bag and tells Monkey that it is full of trouble.

8. Monkey takes the bag out by a tree. When he opens it, a great big dog chases him up a tree.

9. Now Monkey knows that he should not go looking for trouble.

Right There

1. What was the woman baking?

2. What did she spill?

3. Where did she keep her money?

4. Why did she go to the store?

5. What did Monkey think was spilled on the floor?

6. What was in the bag that the grocer gave to Monkey?

Think and Search

Sequence the things that Monkey did from the beginning of the story until the point when he leaves the woman's house to go to the store.

1. He peeks through her window.

2. He watches her stir the batter, drop the molasses, take money from her pocket and leave.

3. He goes into her house and tastes the spilled molasses.

4. He takes money from her apron pocket.

5. He leaves her house and heads to town.

Author and Me

Based on Monkey's behavior, do you think he was a good citizen?

Story Says	I Think	Help Others to See and Understand Your Ideas
He peeks through her window. He watches her stir the batter, drop the molasses, take money from her pocket, and leave. He goes into her house and tastes the spilled molasses. He takes money from her apron pocket. He leaves her house and heads to town.	Monkey is doing a lot of things that a good citizen would never do. Many of the things he is doing are against the law.	A good citizen should have respect for his or her neighbors, and Monkey doesn't seem to have any respect at all. The author says he peeked through her windows. The word *peek* implies that he was being sneaky. He waits for her to leave and then he climbs through the window without permission. Even worse, he steals money from her apron. A good citizen would never break into someone's home. A good citizen would not steal things either. No, Monkey is definitely not a good citizen.

Post-Telling

Lyn Ford's Bag of Trouble

Materials:

1. One lunch-sized paper bag per team

2. Strips of paper or squares of paper large enough for students to write or draw their ideas

3. Pencils, crayons, or fine-point markers

4. Large construction or poster paper, one or two per student

5. Glue or glue sticks

Directions

1. Ask each team to put their names or team number on the bag.

2. Teams now brainstorm types of trouble or draw pictures of trouble, one idea per paper strip. For example: dealing with a bully, difficulty with homework, telling a lie, breaking something that belongs to someone else.

3. Students place their ideas in the team bag.

4. Students now swap bags with another team or work with the ideas in their own bag and discuss the troubles. The goal is for the groups to determine ways to avoid the trouble or ways to improve behavior so that the troubles come to an end.

5. Each team can create a poster of the troubles and the solutions. Add pictures of monkeys, and label the posters with the words from the story: Trouble is not good. Trouble is not sweet. And nobody should go looking for trouble.

Trouble (Add Pictures)	Positive Solutions
Being bothered by a bully	Walk away; find an adult to help you
Feeling angry with a brother or sister	Don't hit them; talk with them and tell them how you feel; talk with your parents
Homework is too difficult	Ask for help; start homework earlier; don't wait until bedtime to do homework
Told a lie	Tell the truth; confess the lie; say you are sorry; remember how bad lying made you feel and don't do it again
Took candy from my brother	Say you are sorry; replace the candy you stole; don't do it again
Eating so much ice cream that I threw up	Use a smaller bowl next time; don't take so much

Additional Sources

Web Sites

Each of these Web sites has additional versions of "Monkey Finds Trouble":

http://www.discover.org.uk/cn/education/documents/MonkeyFindsTrouble.doc (Version from Trinidad)

http://www.scribd.com/doc/15123509/The-Monkey-the-Crocodile

http://www.balagokulam.org/kids/stories/monkeycroc.php ("The Monkey and the Crocodile" is another story about trouble.)

Fairness

Pre-Telling—On My Own

1. Does treating people fairly mean that we should all have to follow the exact same rules?

2. Is it fair if your friends receive more presents at Christmas or birthdays than you do?

3. What does it mean to treat someone with fairness?

"The Theft of Smell," a version by Marilyn Kinsella

Once there was a man who had no job, no home, no family, and very little money. He survived on the goodwill of his fellow villagers, who gave him bits of food. As he walked along the cobblestone roads, he often stopped next to the bakery. Such delicious smells wafted from the open window and into his welcoming nose. On Mondays, he smelled homemade apple pie; on Tuesdays, he smelled sweet doughnuts; on Wednesdays, he smelled yummy meat pies; on Thursdays, he smelled cinnamon cookies; on Fridays, he smelled rich, chocolate cake; and on Saturdays, he smelled the delicious aroma of baking breads.

"Ahh," he said to himself after taking a whiff, "I may have no money, but at least I can enjoy the delicious banquet of aromas." And he closed his eyes and dreamed of eating a royal feast.

One day, while he was taking in the scent of baked bread, the baker came out and saw the man enjoying the aromas of his labors. "What are you doing out here? I thought I smelled a rat! You are stealing my scents."

"What?" cried the poor man. "Stealing your scents . . . makes no sense!"

"We shall see about that," said the baker. "Police, police, come and arrest this man!"

Unfortunately, the poor man was hauled off to jail, where he awaited his trial.

When the day came to meet the judge, the police came and took him by handcuffs to the court. The judge looked down over his wire-rimmed glasses at the two men. "What have we here?"

The baker, still angry, started shouting, "This man, this bum . . . has been stealing from me!"

"I see," said the judge, "and just what has he been taking from you?"

"Everyday this man comes and stands outside my bakery. He never buys anything, and yet, he enjoys my baked goods."

"That is terrible," said the judge, "you mean that he steals your food!"

"Not exactly, Your Honor," said the baker. "In fact, he never even sets foot in the bakery."

"Then, I don't understand. How is he stealing?"

"Well, he smells the aromas of my cooking without paying for them."

"Oh, now I see," said the judge. "He enjoys the scent without paying a single cent!"

"That is correct, Your Honor."

The judge looked at the homeless man and said in a stern voice, "Is this true? You have been accused of the theft of smell. What do have to say for yourself?"

"Your Honor," the man began, "it is true. I do stand outside the bakery. The smells that come from the bakery make me forget my miserable life and, for just a few seconds, I can dream that I am feasting on fine food. I did not know that what I did was wrong."

"I see," said the judge, "but ignorance of the law is no excuse."

The baker nodded and smiled at the judge's wise words.

The judge looked at the baker and said, "To recompense you for this theft, I want this thief to go home and get every bit of money he has and bring it to the court early tomorrow morning." The man was distraught. It was the last of his money, but he did as the judge asked and returned the next morning with a bag filled with assorted coins.

The judge took the bag and said to the baker, "Now, come close." Sneering at the homeless man, the baker approached the bench quickly.

The judge took the bag and shook it vigorously, "Do you hear that?"

"Yes," said the baker as he smiled at the judge.

"Then, that sound is your payment for the theft of smell! And, since you wasted the court's time with such a ridiculous lawsuit, I hereby, declare that you make a baker's dozen of every pastry and donate the thirteenth baked good to the food pantry. That way other poor people cannot only enjoy the aroma, but the taste of your fine ware. So, be it!"

Telling Tips

As students hear this story, they quickly sympathize with the poor man who has been convicted of a crime and ordered to pay a fine. When you are speaking as the judge and reveal the true payment, stress the words *sound* and *smell* so that students grasp the wisdom of the judgment. You can also have some fun with this story with the play on words: *sense, scents,* and *cents.* Play with these lines. You might try saying them normally, or you might try dragging out the words to emphasize the humor.

Story Path

1. A beggar stands outside a bakery and smells the aromas.

2. The baker takes him to court for stealing.

3. After the judge hears both sides, he tells the beggar to go home and bring whatever money he has back to court the next day.

4. The next day the judge takes the bag of coins in his hands and brings the baker to the bench.

5. He shakes the bag of coins and tells him that the sound he hears is the payment for his foolishness.

Right There

1. Where did the beggar stand to "steal the smells?"

2. What kind of smells did he steal?

3. What did the beggar have to bring to the judge the next day?

4. What did the judge say was the payment for the smells?

Think and Search

Can you complete the sequence or the plot of this story?

1. A poor man stands outside the bakery every day enjoying the wonderful scents.

2. One day the baker comes out and accuses the man of _____.

3. The poor man is arrested.

4. The baker and the poor man tell their stories to _____.

5. The judge tells the poor man _____.

6. The next day, _____.

7. The judge tells the baker _____.

Author and Me

1. What lesson do you think the judge wanted the baker to learn from the verdict?

2. What lesson do you think the judge wanted the poor man to learn from the verdict?

3. Why do you think the baker was so angry about the poor man "stealing smell"?

4. Was the final verdict fair?

On My Own

1. How should you treat someone who treats you unfairly?

2. Can you think of some situations that you thought were unfair, but later you realized the situation was not unfair?

3. What could you do if you felt that you were being treated unfairly in a game? In the classroom? At home?

Post-Telling—Freeze Frames

1. The poor man enjoying the scents outside the bakery window.

2. The baker asking the police to arrest the poor man.

3. The baker smiling as the judge orders the poor man to bring his money to court.

4. The baker approaching the judge for his award.

5. The baker learning that he will be given no money and must now bake extra pastries for the poor.

Additional Sources

Books

DeSpain, Pleasant. *Tales of Wisdom and Justice*, Vol. 3. Atlanta, GA: August House, 2001.
    The tales collected in this book are a blend of nonsense stories and wisdom tales from a variety of cultures. Notes on the tales and storytelling suggestions are also provided.

Web Sites

Leslie Slape telling "The Theft of Smell": http://www.youtube.com/watch?v=t-4Aj-AEWyw

Honesty

Pre-Telling—On My Own

1. Did you ever have a time that you did something wrong and wanted to lie about it?

2. What are some reasons that people lie?

3. Is keeping silent about a wrong thing that you have done the same as lying?

4. How does it make you feel to tell the truth?

5. How does it make you feel to lie?

Vocabulary

1. **Mink stole**—a stole is a shawl or a wrap that can be put around the shoulders for warmth. Mink stoles were unusual because the face, tail, and claws of the mink were a part of the stole. At one time, it was considered high fashion to have a stole made from mink fur. At this point it would be helpful to show students a picture of a mink stole or to bring a stole to class if possible.

2. **Rouge**—today we would call this blush; it is a type of makeup used to add color to the cheeks.

"Miss Bessie Loses a Tail," a true story by Marcia Ollinger

Miss Bessie Hayes was a friend of my mother's. She seemed a lot older than my mother. They had worked together in a downtown department store before I was born. Whenever my mother had a ladies' gathering of friends, Miss Bessie would attend. She was a tiny lady with brown curly hair. She always smelled like lilacs or some other fragrant, perfumed flower. She wore lots of rouge on her cheeks and bright red lipstick. She often wore cotton or lace gloves to match her suit, but when she took off her gloves, her hands were covered with large brown spots, like big freckles. One of her favorite bracelets was made from buttons, lots of old buttons, so when she talked and motioned with her hands, the buttons jingled and rattled. But my favorite thing about Miss Bessie Hayes was the way her eyes sparkled with delight whenever she talked to me. I loved Miss Bessie Hayes!

One time, we were at another lady friend's house for a birthday party. Of course, Miss Bessie was there, and she was wearing a mink stole over her pretty suit. When she arrived, she removed the mink stole and placed it on the couch by her purse, where the other ladies had also placed their purses and jackets.

While the ladies sat outside visiting with one another, my girlfriends and I went inside. Soon we spied that mink stole on the couch lying next to the plain cotton sweaters and linen jackets. We stood near the couch staring at that mink. Unable to resist, we let our fingers glide over the silky brown fur; the eyes of the mink seemed to be watching our every move. We decided to try it on. First Jana tried it on, because she was the oldest. "Oh, Dahling, do you like my mink stole?" How rich and elegant it made us feel! As we took turns with the stole, we also held some of the ladies' white lace gloves in our hands and pretended to be all grown up—dressed in our finest.

Next, Jana's little sister, Maureen, tried on the mink. We laughed and giggled and squealed with delight. Finally, it was my turn. I wrapped that mink around my shoulders and dramatically threw one of the tails over my left shoulder. "Look at me. Don't I look fabulous!" But something terrible happened! As I threw the mink tail over my shoulder, it came off! It fell to the floor with a flop.

Our giggling stopped as we stared at the tail of the mink stole lying on the floor. What were we going to do? We considered tucking the tail under the stole and putting it back on the couch and just pretending that nothing had happened. Maureen looked at Jana and then at me. Jana looked right at me. "Marcia, it happened when you put it on, so you have to decide!"

I loved Miss Bessie—her voice, her smell, her dressy look, they way she talked to me and made me feel special. Right then and there, I made my decision. I had to confess. I kept that stole wrapped around my shoulders and marched right out in the backyard where all the ladies were sitting on folding chairs having their party. Jana and Maureen marched right behind me. Holding the fallen tail in my hand, I snuggled up to Miss Bessie. Nearly in tears, I fought to find my voice.

Just as I was about to begin my contrite confession, Miss Bessie said, "Now, my dear Marcia! I see you have been playing with my mink stole. Did he lose one of his tails? Oh, I knew that one was loose, but I thought I could get by wearing it one more time before I would have take it in for repairs. Never you mind, my dear!"

With that, my pounding heart changed to a happy beat. I breathed a big sigh of relief as she gave me a big hug. My face, red as my hair with embarrassment, soon turned back to normal. And my guilt melted away. I was so glad that I had decided to be honest and tell the truth rather than hide the damaged stole. I have never forgotten that day when Miss Bessie lost a tail, and I found the truth in the old saying, "Honesty is the best policy!"

About the Teller

Marcia is a former third-grade teacher who fell in love with storytelling at one of the early St. Louis Storytelling Festivals. Marcia has a master's degree in education and children's literature from the University of Missouri—Columbia. She loves to share her original, traditional, and historical stories with all age groups. You can contact her at storytellermar@aol.com.

Telling Tips

This is a personal experience story told in first person. Normally, tellers do not tell another person's personal experience story, but Marcia has generously given her permission. To share it, tellers must make a choice. They can change it to third person: "Once there was little girl named Marcia, who loved when Miss Bessie came to visit . . . ." Or the teller can keep the story in first person, a more powerful choice that is more connected to the emotional content. To do that, the teller would simply say, "I am going to tell you a story by the author as she would have told it to you." This story is told in a conversational way. Identify the emotional points in the story to make it easier to tell: spying the mink stole on the couch, hearing the tail plop on the floor, making the decision to tell the truth.

You might want to pause after saying this line, "Marcia, it happened when you put it on, so you have to decide!" At this point, ask the students to predict what they think Marcia will do.

Story Path

1. Describe Miss Bessie and why she is so special.

2. Miss Bessie comes to the party wearing her mink stole (admiration).

3. I was playing with it with some girlfriends (happy/silly).

4. A mink tail flew off onto the floor (guilt/shame/sadness).

5. I had to make a decision: put the tail back on and pretend it didn't happen or tell Miss Bessie (thoughtful/struggling).

6. I thought about how much I liked Miss Bessie and decided to be truthful (brave/decisive).

7. Miss Bessie laughed and said it was already loose and that I shouldn't worry about it (relief/happiness).

8. I felt such relief telling the truth (lesson learned).

Right There

1. What was the name of the lady with the mink stole?

2. Who tried on the mink stole?

Think and Search

In the story, the teller gives us a great deal of information about Miss Bessie. What details did the teller share about Miss Bessie (physical appearance, description of makeup and clothing, the special way she made Marcia feel)?

Author and Me

1. Why did Marcia feel so badly about the tail falling off the mink stole?

2. Do you think Marcia made the right decision to tell Miss Bessie?

3. Do you think Marcia would have been honest if Miss Bessie had been an unfriendly person?

On My Own

Let's return to the list of reasons people lie. Can you think of any more reasons why someone might tell a lie? Do any of these reasons justify the lie?

Post-Telling—Freeze Frames

1. Standing at the couch and looking at the stole, deciding if they could touch it.

2. Laughing and giggling as they take turns with it and pretend to be grown up.

3. Staring at the tail lying on the floor.

4. Marching out to tell Miss Bessie.

5. Feeling relief after Miss Bessie says not to worry.

Additional Sources

Books

Bawden, Nina. *Humbug*. New York: Clarion Books, a Houghton Mifflin Company Imprint, 1992.
Cora has been falsely accused of stealing a ring. The story presents numerous opportunities to infer motivation and discuss honesty.

Bunting, Eve. *A Day's Work*. Boston: Houghton Mifflin Harcourt, 1994.
A young boy learns the value of honesty after a hard day of work.

de Paola, Tomie. *Strega Nona*. New York: Simon & Schuster Books for Young Children, 1975.
Based on an Italian tale, this is the story of Big Anthony, whose adolescent mischief causes a great deal of trouble.

Soto, Gary. *Too Many Tamales*. New York: Putnam and Grosset Group, 1993.
A young girl loses her mother's diamond ring. What will she do?

Wojciechowski, Susan, and Susanna Natti. *Don't Call Me Beanhead!* St. Louis, MO: San Val, 1996.
Beany, the worrywart, has failed a test. She takes the advice of Carol Ann, who tells her to hide the F paper inside papers with better grades.

Web Sites

Teacher Tube has a short video with three students discussing whether or not they did their homework. Go to teachertube.com and type honesty into their search engine, or use this link: http://teachertube.com/viewVideo.php?video_id=63722&title=Honesty_Doing_Your_Homework

This Web site has numerous activities and ideas for teaching character education: http://www.goodcharacter.com

Respect

Pre-Telling Activity—On My Own

1. If I were standing on the opposite side of the room and saw you talking with someone, how would I know that you were talking with someone that you respect? What might I see? What might I hear?

2. What might I see if you were being disrespectful? What might I hear?

3. Is it disrespectful to play jokes on people? Or to trick people?

Respect	
Question	**Examples**
What does respect look like?	Hold the door for someone, pick up something someone drops, look them in the eye and smile
What does respect sound like?	Please, thank you, how are you today, hello
How does respect feel?	A warm feeling, safe
What does respect never look like?	Hateful face, ignoring someone, rolling eyes or making a face behind someone's back
What does respect never sound like?	Laughing at someone's problems, making fun of someone behind his/her back
How does respect never feel?	Hurtful, embarrassing

"Reef Eyes," a folktale from Namdrik Atoll in the Marshall Islands, told by Iban Edwin, adapted by Daniel A. Kelin, II

On the tiny island of Namdrik, two young girls played tricks on everyone and everything. The two girls loved to sit in coconut trees and drop big brown coconuts on everyone walking by. They would laugh and laugh. The two girls enjoyed greasing the ceiling and walls of their house with coconut oil so that tiny geckos scuttling by slipped and plopped to the floor. They would laugh and laugh. At night, the two girls liked tip-toeing into the dark to grab the leg of a sleeping pig. They would pull until it squealed loud enough to wake everyone on the island. The two girls always laughed and laughed.

Mama and Papa scolded their two naughty girls. "Stop playing tricks on everyone and everything," the parents told them. "Someday, you're going to get into trouble that you can't get out of."

Did the girls listen to their parents? Of course not! Instead they decided to play their biggest trick ever. This is what happened.

The chief of the island paddled in from the ocean one morning with a big load of fish. He had snagged a giant pile of his favorite fish. He piled all the fish in front of his house. Tired out, the chief decided to take a short nap. When he woke up, the chief felt like cooking up those delicious fish. But stepping out of his house, he got an unwelcome surprise. "What happened to my fish?" the chief shouted.

A burst of giggles rustled the trees above him. Looking up through the leaves, he saw the two young girls. "It was you two!"

"We never saw your fish," said the first girl.

"We're just collecting coconuts for Mama and Papa," answered the second.

"I know you two. You stole my fish," he yelled. "I want them back right now."

"Right now?" the two girls asked and smiled.

"Right this very moment," the chief growled.

"Okay." The two girls shook the tree. Fish rained down. The chief ran into his house to keep from getting slapped by all those fish. But he had caught a huge bunch of fish, and the roof of his house caved in, burying him.

The two girls slid down the tree and skipped off, laughing. The chief wasn't laughing. He struggled out of the pile of fish and house. The chief took a deep breath, and then let out a furious roar.

The roar echoed across the tiny island. The two girls nearly leapt out of their skins. They begged their parents to help them. "Please, please, please, hide us!" Did their parents help? No way.

The girls ran to the other islanders. "He's after us. Help!" Did the islanders help? No way.

The two even pleaded with the geckos and pigs. "Help, the chief is chasing us!" Did the geckos and pigs help? No way. In fact, one pig waddled away, just giving them attitude.

The roaring grew closer. The girls took off running. The chief roared on and ran right after them.

The girls sprinted to the very end of the island. The two frantically looked for a place to hide. Not a bit of land was left, just a horizon full of ocean. The girls felt trapped. The chief's roaring grew louder every second. The two girls looked at each other, fear filling their eyes. What could they do? And then they saw it. At the edge of the reef sat a huge clam with its mouth wide open, basking in the sun. The two girls leapt into the clam. They slammed it shut. Just four wide eyes peaked out as the girls waited nervously for the furious chief.

The chief roared right to the end of the island. Breathing heavily, he hunted for those two little tricksters. He found nothing. And as hard as he listened, he didn't hear even a single giggle. "Just wait until I find you two," the chief said and marched off.

The two girls laughed. "What a great trick we played on the . . . ." They pushed to open the clam. It was stuck. The girls pounded, kicked, and shoved at the giant shell, but it refused to open even a crack. The two girls quit laughing. They never got out.

And to this day in the Marshall Islands, that kind of clam is called a *mejanwod*, which means "reef eyes."

Iban Edwin, "Reef Eyes," recorded and translated by Daniel A. Kelin, II, reprinted from *Highlights for Children*, Vol. 57, No. 4 (April 2002), pp. 11–13. Copyright © 2002 by Highlights for Children, Inc.

About the Teller

Daniel Kelin, who holds an MFA in child drama from the University of Hawaii, serves as the director of drama education for the Honolulu Theatre for Youth. As a 2009 Fulbright research scholar, he spent six months in schools in India to implement an integrated program of drama, history, and culture. An award-winning writer, Dan's most recent book is *In Their Own Words: Drama with Young English Language Learners*. Recognized as a Master Teaching Artist, he has served as a trainer in Applied Theatre with JNJIE, a Marshall Islands youth organization. His long association with the Marshalls led to his book *Marshall Islands Legends and Stories*. Find out more at http://www.DanielAKelin.com.

Telling Tips

This is a story from the Marshall Islands. If you wish to tell it as a folktale from that area, then you should get a feel for the islands—where they are located, the people who live there, and how they live. If you tell this as a Marshall Island story, you must be true to the characters and objects in the story. You can, however, take the idea of the story and relocate it. It would no longer be a Marshall Island story, but rather an "adapted" story.

Story Path

1. Once there were two girls who made others angry with their pranks, but they just laughed it off.

2. The parents warned them that something bad would happen if they kept doing it.

3. One day, they took the load of fish that the chief had in front of his house and placed them in the tree.

4. When the chief couldn't find the fish, the girls said they didn't know where the fish were. When the chief went back inside, the girls shook the fish from the tree, and it hit the chief's roof. It collapses.

5. The chief knew that they were lying and chased them down to the beach.

6. Along the way, the girls asked for help from others who declined, because the girls had often played mean tricks on them.

7. The girls hid in a giant clam.

8. Not finding them, the chief left.

9. When the girls tried to get out of the clam, they couldn't. Today they still live in clams as reef eyes to remind others what can happen when you show disrespect.

Right There

1. What is the setting for this story?

2. What do the girls do after every prank that they pull?

3. Whose fish did the girls hide?

4. Where did the girls end up hiding when they were being chased?

Think and Search

1. Make a list of the tricks that the girls pulled.

2. Who did the girls turn to for help when the chief was chasing them?

Author and Me

1. How do you think the people of the island felt about these two girls?

2. What choices did the girls make throughout the story that led to their final problem of becoming reef eyes?

3. Do you think that turning the girls into "reef eyes" was a fair punishment? Why or why not?

Post-Telling

1. Return to the chart that was created during the On My Own session. Have students add more ideas about respect.

2. Divide the students into small groups. Give each group a behavior of the girls and have the group brainstorm the effect or outcome of the girls' behavior. A sample is provided.

Cause–Behavior	Effect–Outcome
The girls dropped coconuts on people's heads, and then they laughed and laughed.	1. People were physically hurt by the coconut. 2. People were embarrassed by the laughing. 3. People did not like the girls. 4. The girls earned a reputation as tricksters who hurt people. 5. People would not help the girls when the chief was chasing them. Perhaps they thought it was another trick.
The girls greased the ceiling and walls of their house with coconut oil so that tiny geckos scuttling by slipped and plopped to the floor.	
The girls would tip-toe into the dark to grab the leg of a sleeping pig. They would pull until it squealed loud enough to wake everyone on the island.	
The girls refused to listen to their parents.	
The girls hid the chief's fish and then dropped them from a coconut tree, causing the roof of his house to collapse on top of him.	

Dan Kelin's Snapshots

As a class, make a list of the story's characters. Students will now create "Snapshots," or individual frozen statues, of the characters as follows.

1. Students stand in a neutral position (feet together, hands at their side, facing forward) in their own personal space.

2. Call out prompt, such as, "How can you shape/freeze your body to look like . . .

   • the girls throwing coconuts?"

   • the girls laughing?"

   • the islanders getting hit by coconuts?"

   • the parents, upset?"

   • the chief, fishing?"

   • the chief, surprised when his fish have disappeared?"

   • the pig giving attitude?"

   • the chief roaring?"

   • the girls stuck in the clam?"

3. Allow three to five seconds for students to shape their bodies into a frozen image and then call "Snapshot."

4. Without naming any students, describe what you see that is an effective snapshot. Explain what you see that lets you infer the feelings of the character in the story. Imitate some of the snapshots that you see so that students understand the benchmarks for creating an effective snapshot.

5. Provide an opportunity for students to create new snapshots by repeating steps 1 through 3.

6. After students have had an opportunity to try two or three snapshots, select a few students to create snapshots for the rest of the class to see. Have students explain what they see that enables them to infer the feelings of the characters. Point out the subtle use of facial expressions or the positioning of the hands or body that allow us to make an inference.

Post-Telling—Freeze Frames

1. The girls planning a trick.

2. One girl picking on the pig.

3. The parents scolding the girls (how the girls feel).

4. The girls reacting to the fish falling on the chief.

5. The girls reacting to the chief's roar.

6. The girls begging for help from the parents.

7. The chief looking for the hiding girls.

Additional Sources

Books (additional titles from the storyteller)

Kelin, Daniel A., II. *In Their Own Words: Drama with Young English Language Learners*. Charlotte, NC: New Plays, 2009.

Kelin, Daniel A., II. *Marshall Islands Legends and Stories*. Honolulu, HI: Bess Press, 2003.

Both are available at: http://www.dramaticpublishing.com/p2176/In-Their-Own-Words:-Drama-With-Young-English-Language-Learners/product_info.html

Web Sites

en.wikipedia.org/wiki/Marshall Islands

http://www.360cities.net/area/marshall-islands

http://www.getahugetank.com/giant-clam-pacific-p-2440.html

http://www.fotosearch.com/UNS022/u13489701/

en.wikipedia.org/wiki/File:Giant_clam_or_Tridacna_gigas.jpg

Drama Activities

http://www.prel.org/eslstrategies/drama.html

Responsibility

Pre-Telling—On My Own

It takes a lot of people to make a school a safe and happy place. People in our school do many jobs. Let's think about some of the people we see at school every day and find out if we know what their responsibilities are. What might our day be like if the people didn't do their jobs responsibly?

Person	List of Responsibilities	What Are the Consequences If People Shirk Their Responsibilities?
Janitor		
Cooks		
Classroom Line Leaders		
Bus Drivers		
Classroom Door Holders		

After completing the chart ask: What are the characteristics of responsible people? Suggestions:

- They accept jobs and tasks.
- They work to complete tasks without anyone nagging them or reminding them over and over.
- They know their strengths and abilities.
- They use talents to accomplish things.
- They don't blame others if they fail at a task.
- They think before doing something.

Verb Poem

Let students interview some people in your school to determine what types of responsibilities each job entails. Following the interview, create a verb poem about that person. The title of the person is the title of the poem. Every line of the poem begins with a verb describing a responsibility of the person. Make posters with pictures of the individual and the verb poem. This can be done before or after the discussion of the story. Following is a sample verb poem:

The School Secretary
Keeps track of lunch money
Takes phone calls
Types letters
Fixes the copy machine
Greets visitors
Orders school supplies
Makes announcements
Locks doors
Tells the principal what to do
Our school secretary—Responsibility in Action

"Little Bird," as told by Janet Pacella Jones

Today we are going to hear a story about a bird that learned the importance of using her talents to do her job in a responsible manner.

Long ago, before there were people on earth, the animals were all learning their places in the world. They were all choosing jobs that would let them use their special talents. All were learning, except Little Bird.

"Now, Bird," said the Sun, "you will need to decide what you are going to do in this world by the time I rise tomorrow morning, or I am going to take you back into the clouds with me. Do you understand?"

"I understand," Bird twittered. "I promise I will decide and let you know. Yes, yes, I will."

"Alright, then," said Sun, "I'm depending on you."

Bird flew off wondering what in the world she could choose. As she flew, she looked down at the faraway ground and spotted Cat licking herself.

"What shall I do? What shall I do? Shall I lick my paws just like you?" chirped Bird.

"Silly Bird, you have no paws, but I would be happy to eat you for my lunch," said Cat hungrily.

"Oh, noooo, thank you. I must be going," said Bird, and she flew off to continue her journey. Soon, she was flying over a rippling brook where a fish swam, its glittering scales shining in the sun.

"What shall I do? What shall I do? Shall I swim in the brook just like you?" asked Bird.

"You can try," gurgled Fish. Bird began to swim, but all she could do was flap her wings and sputter in the water. She wasn't getting anywhere.

"Thank you, Fish. I admire you greatly, but I am not a swimmer. I must be going now," and she flew off again.

After a while, Bird noticed a squirrel with its cheeks full of food.

"What shall I do? What shall I do? Shall I gather nuts just like you?"

"You can try," said Squirrel with her mouth so full she could hardly talk. Bird did try but all she could gather were small berries and seeds. She knew she would never save enough for the winter this way.

"Thank you, Squirrel. Gathering food is important work, no doubt, but I cannot do it," said Bird, and she flew off once again.

By now, it was dark and Bird was getting worried. She must find a special job that she could do before Sun rose the next morning. Then, she heard Owl singing a song. "Whooo, whooo," said Owl. Suddenly, Bird knew what she had to do. All night long, she worked on a song. It was not Owl's song but her own Bird song. It went like this:

"I'm looking for a song to call my very own.
A song that will last my whole life long then I'll never be alone."

When Sun came up, he heard Bird singing and said, "Bird, what a wonderful song! You have found your work. From now on, you will sing to all the other animals."

And to this day, Bird sings to us every morning.

About the Teller

Janet has told stories for eighteen years. She holds master's degrees in music and education (curriculum and instruction) and has taught piano to all ages for thirty years. Janet can be reached at janetjones437@gmail.com.

Telling Tips

This is an original "How and Why Story" that explains why birds chirp in the mornings. It sets up a problem (Bird has no special talent to bring to the world). It goes on a journey to find that talent (meets Cat, Fish, Squirrel, and Owl). Bird finds her own talent (singing). The problem is solved, and that explains why birds sing in the morning. This story has a refrain: "What shall I do? What shall I do?" Practice this ahead of time. At first, have the students do a call and response. Then, have a hand gesture that indicates it's time for them to say the line. Remind them that every time you do the hand gesture, they need to repeat the line. The line after the refrain changes each time, so the teller needs to say that line without the group. Feel free to sing the bird's final song. Make up a melody and sing; have fun with it.

Story Path

1. Sun tells Bird it must find its contribution to the world or it will have to leave.

2. Bird goes to Cat (licking paws)—no paws.

3. Then Bird goes to Fish (swimming)—can't swim.

4. Then she goes to Squirrel (carrying nuts)—mouth too small.

5. Bird hears Owl hooting and realizes her special talent for singing her own song.

6. Sun is pleased and allows Bird to stay on earth to sing in the mornings.

Right There

1. What did Cat say that made the Bird leave so suddenly?

2. Bird couldn't carry nuts in her mouth like Squirrel, but what could it carry?

3. What was Owl's song?

Think and Search

This charming little story loosely follows Aristotle's "Hero Cycle," a common plot structure for many coming of age stories. Have students trace the cycle of the story and compare it to other coming-of-age stories.

Story Element of Hero Cycle	Evidence of Story Element in Little Bird
The hero is given a reason to leave his or her safe environment and go out into the world on an adventure.	Little Bird is told she must find a purpose in life.
The hero faces a series of challenges.	Little Bird encounters the cat, the fish, the squirrel, and the owl.
The hero changes or gains maturity and can now return home.	Little Bird discovers her song which gives her a purpose in life.

Author and Me

1. Why didn't the little Bird just copy the Owl's song note for note?

2. Did Bird act responsibly in this story?

On My Own

1. What kind of responsibilities do you have in your life?

2. How do you know if you are being a responsible person?

3. How are the responsibilities that you have now different than the responsibilities you had as a first grader?

Post-Telling—Freeze Frames

1. Little Bird is told she must find purpose in life.

2. Little Bird encounters the cat.

3. Little Bird encounters the fish.

4. Little Bird encounters the squirrel.

5. Little Bird encounters the owl.

6. Little Bird discovers her purpose in life.

Additional Sources

Books

Kipling, Rudyard. *Just So Stories*. Mineola, NY: Dover Publications, 2001.
    This is perhaps the most famous collection of how and why stories. Students will enjoy the humor, magic, and strange happenings as they discuss these inspiring stories of creation.

Williams, Vera. *A Chair for My Mother*. New York: HarperCollins, 1984.
    This simple picture book tells the story of a young girl, her mother, and grandmother who save their spare coins to buy an easy chair after having lost everything in a fire. It is a deep look at poverty, social justice, and responsibility.

Web Sites

http://www.learner.org/jnorth/tm/loon/Legends.html

http://www.acpl.lib.in.us/children/howandwhy.html

Scholastic Instructor— activities that explore other cultures and integrate language arts and science: http://teacher.scholastic.com/products/instructor/pourquoitales.htm

Native American stories online: http://www.ilhawaii.net/~stony/loreindx.html

Aristotle's "Hero Cycle": http://www.skotos.net/articles/TTnT_76.shtml

Chapter 5

Stories, QARs, and Activities for Grades 5 and 6

See Chapter 3 for instructions and samples of all activities.

Caring

Pre-Telling—On My Own

1. What would you wear to go to a football game?

2. What would you wear to go a concert with a group of friends?

3. What would you wear if you were going to the White House to receive an award?

4. Why do we wear different outfits for different occasions?

Vocabulary

Mitzvah: a Hebrew term that refers to an act of human kindness; showing respect and care for everyone; not judging another

Predict-O-Gram

Provide students with the following words. Provide definitions as needed. The task is for them to assign the words to one of the following categories: character, setting, or plot. Students must determine whether they think the word represents a character in the story, if it is a setting, or if it will be an element that moves the plot forward. Because students are not yet familiar with the story, they are using their background knowledge of character, setting, and plot to determine the assignment of words. This is an On My Own activity.

Joshua	a rich boy	red velvet robe	a grand home
mud	*mitzvah* ice cream		

Discuss their decisions to determine their line of reasoning for the assignments they have made. The goal is *not* for them to assign everything with 100-percent accuracy. The goal is to assess their understanding of character, setting, and plot. After hearing the story, students will return to their assignments to decide whether they want to make any changes to their original predictions. At this point, the students will also take all words assigned to plot and determine whether the word is part of the problem or part of the solution. (Adapted from Blachowicz 1986, 643–649).

"The Red Velvet Robe," or "Feed My Clothes," a traditional Jewish folktale as told by Diann Joy Bank

Jacob and Sarah were proud of their son, Joshua. They had taught him to do a *mitzvah* each day—to be kind and respectful of others. Although they had little money for fine clothes or an elegant home, Joshua took good care of his simple clothes. He grew to the age of ten and was known throughout the community for his good ways.

One day, a wealthy family moved to town, and they invited all of the town's children to come to a party at their grand home to meet their son. Excited to go to the party and meet the new boy, Joshua put on his one good outfit. Though his shirt was a bit faded, his clothes were clean and pressed; they had no tears or rips. Joshua walked to the rich boy's home, and as he walked, he waved at neighbors and called friendly greetings to all he met. He soaked in the warmth of the midday sun.

Before long, he reached the boy's home and headed toward the front door. Suddenly, a large rain cloud appeared over his head and poured down upon Joshua. The gush of rain created mud puddles, and Joshua rushed toward the front door in an attempt to stay dry and clean. He slipped and fell into a puddle; he was covered from top to bottom in mud.

Joshua thought, "I'll get help to clean up inside." He knocked, and a servant opened the door. Joshua could see a boy sitting at a fancy table; he wore a gold jacket and pants. Seeing Joshua covered in mud, this boy yelled, "Send away that dirty boy in those terrible clothes. The way he is dressed, he cannot be one of my honored guests!" And with that the servant immediately slammed the door in Joshua's face.

Joshua quickly returned home to his parents. "What happened to you?" his parents asked.

"The new boy wouldn't let me tell him about my falling in the mud puddle outside his door. Before I could explain, they slammed the door in my face. He saw my muddy clothes and said that I could not be an honored guest."

Joshua's mother thought for a moment, and then opened her dresser drawer. "Take this beautiful robe of red velvet, the silk shirt, and these velvet pants. We were saving these clothes for you for a special holiday," smiled his mother. "Today, these clothes will serve you well."

Joshua returned to the boy's house. This time he carefully avoided the mud puddles and knocked on the front door. The servant once again opened the door. The rich boy now welcomed Joshua saying, "What a fine robe you are wearing. Clearly, your clothes make you special; I know that you must be one of my honored guests. Come sit next to me at the table." All of the guests admired Joshua's clothes. "Let the party begin," commanded the boy.

Joshua sat next to the boy, but he did not say one word. He looked across the long table filled with luscious food. Joshua reached for the sweet red drink at his place and poured it down the front of his white silk shirt. "Enjoy! Enjoy!" he said to his clothes.

The new boy and his guests stared at Joshua but said nothing. Next, Joshua picked up the baked chicken, the mashed potatoes, and the string beans and rubbed them up and down his velvet pants. "Enjoy! Enjoy!" Joshua said speaking to his clothes.

The new boy's face turned bright red, and his eyes bulged from his head. Then Joshua took a bowl of ice cream and swirled it all over his red velvet robe. "Enjoy! Enjoy!" he told his clothes once again.

"What kind of manners are these?" the boy screamed.

Joshua, looking straight into the bulging eyes of the boy, finally spoke. "The first time that I came to your celebration, I had fallen into the mud outside your door. Before I could speak, you said, 'Send away that dirty boy in those terrible clothes. The way he is dressed, he cannot be one of my honored guests!' And then your servant slammed the door in my face."

"When I returned in my fancy clothes, you said, 'Clearly, your clothes make you special; I know that you are one of my honored guests.' Then you invited me to sit next to you. I knew then that you had invited my fancy clothes to dinner, not me. So, I decided to feed my red velvet robe and clothes. I do not see any *mitzvah* of kindness at this table."

Joshua returned home dripping of food all over his clothes. After he told his parents what had happened, they helped him to repair the damage to his fancy clothes. They knew that their son understood the importance of doing a *mitzvah* and to always welcome and honor all your guests, not just their clothes.

About the Teller

Diann Joy Bank, professional storyteller and educator, employs audience participation in her storytelling performances and workshops. In her published works, *Grandma Annie's Gourmet Delights* and "The Negune Tune" in the book *First Harvest, Jewish Writing in St. Louis*, she evokes our imaginations to teach values from her multicultural and Jewish folklore centered on character development themes. With her experience as a teacher in early childhood, an ESL teacher, and assistant teacher in elementary schools, Diann would be delighted to share her stories with you. Contact her at dbanktells@sbcglobal.net or visit her Web site: www.diannjoybank.net.

Telling Tips

This is an original version of a Jewish folktale. It is a story that encourages actions from the teller. Pretend to be the boy pouring the drink on his shirt. Don't be afraid to exaggerate as you imitate him rubbing the clothes on his robe and pants. This odd behavior will likely confuse your listeners as much as it confused the wealthy boy sitting at the table watching the spectacle.

Story Path

1. Introduce Jacob, Sarah, and their son Joshua and explain why they are proud of their son.

2. Joshua is invited to the party and walks to the new boy's house.

3. He falls into the mud when a sudden storm arrives.

4. He is sent away because of his appearance.

5. Joshua returns home to explain why he was rejected.

6. The mother presents him with new clothes that she had been saving.

7. Joshua returns and is given a seat of honor near the new boy.

8. Joshua pours a drink on his shirt and then rubs food into his velvet pants saying, "Enjoy!"

9. Now Joshua swirls ice cream on his robe, and the other boy yells at him.

10. Joshua explains why he is feeding his clothes and returns home.

Right There

1. What is a *mitzvah*?

2. Why was Joshua not allowed into the rich boy's home the first time?

Think and Search

1. Compare the two receptions that Joshua received each time he rang the doorbell of the rich boy's home.

2. List the behaviors and actions that the wealthy boy displays throughout the story.

Author and Me

1. Do you agree with Joshua's method of teaching the rich boy a lesson about *mitzvah*?

2. What other ways might Joshua have tried to make his point to the rich boy?

3. If Joshua had not fallen into the mud, how do you think the rich boy would have received him when he arrived at the house in his faded clothes?

On My Own

1. Do you think it is right or wrong to judge people based on the clothes they wear?

2. Think about someone in your life who is caring. How does that person show that he or she cares for others?

Post-Telling

Create an *I Am* poem from the viewpoint of one of the character's in the story: Joshua, the wealthy boy, a guest at the table, the servant who opened the door both times, or Joshua's parents.

Predict-O-Gram

Return to the predictions students made before hearing the story. Now students will assign the words to the following categories: character, setting, problem, resolution.

Joshua	a rich boy	red velvet robe	a grand home
mud	*mitzvah*	ice cream	

Additional Sources

Books

Sadeh, Pinhas. Hillel Halkin, translator. *Jewish Folktales.* New York: Knopf Doubleday, 1989. The book contains more than two hundred stories drawn from Eastern Europe and Africa. The number of stories will give the teller a range of choices. The book includes an afterword by Sadeh, who offers insights and interpretations for many of the tales.

Web Sites

This site offers an extensive list of books that have other Jewish folktales: http://www.jewishlibraries.org/ajlweb/resources/bib_bank/OaklandUFolktales.pdf

Citizenship

Pre-Telling—On My Own

Anticipation Guide

Before		After
	Good citizens must sometimes put aside their own wants and needs in order to make life better for everyone in the community.	
	Being a good citizen means having total faith in authorities.	
	Good citizens can recognize imperfections or faults in their country, but also love their country.	
	Good citizens always follow the law.	
	Sometimes it is difficult to be a good citizen.	
	Children cannot practice citizenship because they are not old enough to vote or run for public office.	
	Because the government protects our rights, we have an obligation to be good citizens.	
	Studying American history helps people to be better citizens.	
	Citizenship is a synonym for American.	

Vocabulary: bonded laborer, collateral, rupees, liberation, sanctions, mafia

"Iqbal Masih: Human Rights Worker," researched and written by Kate Dudding

Some people say "Children cannot make a real difference in the world." I am going to tell you a true story about one child who did make a real difference.

His name was Iqbal Masih. Between the ages of ten and twelve, he led thousands of children to freedom. He spoke in front of large meetings of children. He told them his story. He urged them, "Come with me and be free." Thousands of children followed him to freedom.

Iqbal's story was very much like the stories of the children to whom he spoke. Iqbal was born to a poor family in Pakistan; his father was a laborer and his mother, a housecleaner. When Iqbal was two, his father deserted the family. Later, when Iqbal's older brother was getting married, the father, even though he had deserted his family, knew that he must still pay for part of the festivities. But he did not have the money, and as a poor laborer, he could not get a loan from a bank. So he borrowed 600 rupees ($12) from the owner of the nearby carpet factory. The father used Iqbal as the collateral for the loan; Iqbal would have to work in the carpet factory until the debt was paid. He became a bonded laborer.

Iqbal was only four years old at the time, and the year was 1987.

Iqbal worked in an airless room with twenty looms and one small bare light bulb. All the windows were sealed to keep out insects that might damage the wool used to make carpets.

Later Iqbal told people, "I started working when I was four. I used to leave my home at four o'clock in the morning and come back at seven o'clock at night. That happened six days a week. I only had energy to play on my one day off. I was often chained to my loom. I was fed a meager lunch which I had to pay for. Sometimes I would sneak away, but I would get beaten on my return."

Children were not allowed to speak to each other in the factory. Iqbal later told his listeners, "The factory owner told us, if the children spoke, they were not giving their complete attention to the product and were likely to make errors."

During one of the times that Iqbal snuck away from the factory, he went to the police station to report the threats, beatings, and other terrible conditions. The policemen returned Iqbal to the factory where he was given a terrible beating and told, "You are a working boy, a carpet weaver; you will remain a carpet weaver for the rest of your life."

There was no escape; no end to the work. Members of Iqbal's family kept borrowing from the carpet factory owner. The original 600 rupee debt ($12) grew to 13,000 rupees ($260)—too much to ever be paid off.

Finally, wonderful things started happening in 1993, the year Iqbal turned ten.

Pakistan's parliament passed a law that abolished bonded labor contracts and canceled all debts owed because of bonded labor. All the bonded laborers had to do was present a "freedom letter" to their factory owners, declaring the termination of their bonded labor contracts. Penalty for loaning money in return for bonded labor was now a minimum of two years in jail plus stiff fines.

Realizing that most bonded laborers could not read newspapers and probably did not know about the new law, Eshan Ullah Khan and other members of an organization called the Bonded Labor Liberation Front (BLLF) of Pakistan traveled from village to village, holding meetings and rallies, explaining the new law. The BLLF wanted to help all bonded laborers. They would help to free children like Iqbal.

Iqbal's carpet factory owner warned all of his workers to stay away from the BLLF rally in their village. Iqbal thought, "If my factory owner said something was bad, then it must be good." The factory owner had threatened Iqbal, but that day he ran away from work anyway. For the first time, Iqbal learned that a new law canceled his family's debt to the carpet factory owner.

Eshan Ullah Khan, a speaker for BLLF, spotted Iqbal at that rally and brought him up on stage, asking him to introduce himself, to give his name, his age, the carpet factory owner's name, and the amount of his debt. Everyone was stunned that Iqbal was ten years old; he looked six. His growth and physical development had been stunted from malnutrition and long hours of leaning over his loom.

After the meeting, Iqbal refused to return to work until a BLLF lawyer wrote a freedom letter for him. Iqbal insisted on delivering that letter in person because he wanted to tell the other boys, "Come with me and be free." The factory owner was furious but could do nothing.

Iqbal started attending school for the first time, a Bonded Labor Liberation Front school, and traveled to meetings with Eshan Ullah Khan, urging children to "Come with me and be free."

Iqbal became the first recipient of Reebok's Youth in Action Human Rights Award. As part of the award, Iqbal visited Boston, Massachusetts, for one week in December 1994. While there, he visited the Broad Meadows Middle School in Quincy, Massachusetts. His translator became exhausted translating all of Iqbal's talks and conversations. The students crowded together and even stood on chairs at lunch just to catch a better glimpse of Iqbal.

Later that week, during his acceptance speech for the Reebok award, Iqbal told his story. "In my country, children work with this instrument (holding up his carpet tool). Children need this instrument (holding up a pen)." He asked President Clinton to put sanctions on countries using child labor.

Later, when asked what he wanted to be when he grew up, Iqbal replied, "A lawyer, fighting for the rights of my people. But first I have to finish school."

Unfortunately, Iqbal never finished school. Four months after receiving the Reebok award, while riding a bicycle with his cousin, Iqbal was shot dead. There were many investigations into his death. His murderer is still unknown; perhaps it was a crazed villager or perhaps a member of the carpet mafia in Pakistan.

But, amazingly, this is *not* the end of Iqbal's story.

In the two years after Iqbal's death, the students at Broad Meadows Middle School used the Internet and e-mail to contact middle school students around the world. They raised money from three thousand school and youth groups in all fifty states and twenty-seven countries. They suggested a $12 gift, symbolic of Iqbal's age at his death and the original debt. Students donated $127,000, and $19,000 more from Reebok, unions, celebrities, and other adults. With the total of $146,000, a school was built in Pakistan in Iqbal's honor.

In Canada, twelve-year-old Craig Kielburger read a newspaper article about Iqbal after Iqbal's death. With friends, Craig started Free the Children (www.freethechildren.com). In the eleven years after Iqbal's death alone, this organization built four hundred schools and raised $9 million for medical supplies.

Two and a half years after Iqbal's death, President Clinton signed a law making it illegal to import goods created by bonded child labor.

Some people say, "Children cannot make a real difference in the world." I guess those people have never heard of the students at Broad Meadows Middle School, or Craig Kielburger, or Iqbal Masih.

About the Teller

Storyteller and writer Kate Dudding (B.A. in psychology and French, M.S. in computer science) enjoys bringing history to life—giving a voice to people from the past. Her first CD, *Lighting the Way Home: Stories of Lighthouses and Their Keepers*, is a Parents' Choice Approved Award Winner of 2007, one of six storytelling CDs to receive an award that year. Her story about Iqbal Masih is also on her second CD, *People Who Made a Difference, Volume 1*, and received a 2010 Storytelling World Honor Award for preadolescent listeners. Find out more at http://www.katedudding.com.

Telling Tips

This is a true story that has been carefully researched and written by the teller. It is important to stay true to the facts of the story. Be careful to identify the characters so that students do not confuse members of the BLLF with the owner of the factory. Students need to understand that the BLLF was working to help Iqbal. Numerous quotes from Iqbal are used throughout the story to provide a sense of Iqbal's sense of strength and dedication to helping others.

Story Path

1. Background on Iqbal and how he became a bonded laborer.

2. Iqbal's working conditions: long hours, six days a week, no access to fresh air, chained to his loom, meager lunch, not allowed to speak, beatings, and threats.

3. Worsening conditions: no help from the police, and Iqbal's family's original debt continued to grow.

4. 1993—Pakistan passed the law abolishing bonded labor and freeing bonded laborers.

5. Formation of the BLLF and their goals to help people.

6. Iqbal warned to stay away from rally.

7. Eshan Ullah Khan of BLLF spots Iqbal and has him speak to the crowd; the people who see him are amazed at his poor physical health.

8. Iqbal stands up to the factory owner and invites children to "Come with me and be free."

9. Iqbal receives Reebok award and travels the United States speaking to large audiences. He shows the carpet tool and the pen and begs President Clinton to sanction countries using child labor.

10. Iqbal is killed while riding a bike.

11. Broad Meadows Middle School asks people for $12 to help build schools.

12. Craig Kielburger began Free the Children which has raised $9 million to build schools.

13. President Clinton signed a law making it illegal to import goods created by bonded child labor.

Right There

1. Where did Iqbal live?

2. Why was Iqbal working in the carpet factory?

3. How many days a week did Iqbal work in the carpet factory?

4. How old was Iqbal when he became a bonded laborer?

5. How old was he when he was freed from bonded labor?

6. How did the children at Broad Meadows Middle School learn about Iqbal?

7. How did Craig Kielburger learn about Iqbal?

Think and Search

1. What hardships did Iqbal suffer as a bonded laborer?

2. Explain what it means to be a bonded laborer.

3. What good things happened after Iqbal's death?

Author and Me

1. What do you think gave Iqbal the strength to stand up to the factory owners?

2. Which people in this story demonstrated the qualities of citizenship? What qualities did they demonstrate?

Post-Telling

After a discussion of the story using the QAR, return to the Anticipation Guide. Allow students time to mark their post-telling answers and then discuss them.

Metaphors and Similes for Citizenship

Example 1: Citizenship *is a treadmill.* Sometimes we do not want to use the treadmill because it is difficult. If a person uses the treadmill only when it is convenient, it doesn't do much good. But the person who uses it every day becomes stronger and healthier. It is the same with citizenship. Sometimes it is difficult to be a good citizen. If a person practices being a good citizen only when it is convenient, it doesn't amount to much. But if a person practices being a good citizen every day, the community will be stronger and healthier.

Example 2: Being a good citizen is *like being a member of a chorus*; everyone's voice must be heard to create beautiful music.

Example 3: A list poem

> *Citizenship is like jogging.*
> *Practice daily*
> *You become stronger*
> *You become healthier*
> *It's not always easy*
> *It's not always fun*
> *But it is always beneficial*
> *Citizenship is like jogging.*

Additional Sources

Books

Kinsey-Warnock, Natalie. *The Night the Bells Rang*. New York: Puffin Books, 2000.

> This is a story of two young boys who lived in Vermont in 1918. Aden, the town bully, risks his life to do something good for Mason. Aden then goes off to war and is killed in action. When armistice is announced, the town celebrates by giving every citizen a chance to ring the church bell. At this point, Mason must deal with his feelings toward Aden.

Kuklin, Susan. *Iqbal Masih and the Crusaders against Child Slavery*. New York: Henry Holt, 1998.

Web Sites

A history of how Craig Kielburger learned of Iqbal and founded Free the Children: http://www. freethechildren.com/aboutus/ftchistory.php.

A Web site about Iqbal and Broadmeadow Middle School students: http://www.mirrorimage. com/iqbal.

Youth Service America offers grants for community improvement, lesson plans, and ideas for service projects: http://www.ysa.org.

Fairness

Pre-Telling—On My Own

1. Many species of animals are being placed on the endangered list. Why is this happening? What is endangering the animals?

2. Is it fair to the next generation that some animals may no longer exist?

3. Can you think of other situations in which animals are treated unfairly?

Situation in which animals are treated unfairly	Why do you think that this is unfair to the animals?	Is there a way to prevent this problem?

Background information for the story: In the lowlands of Senegal, cheetahs roam freely, but their numbers are diminishing. Their natural habitat is being destroyed by the need for farmland, the growth of towns, poaching, and the spread of disease. These shy, swift cats are struggling to survive in a rapidly progressing world. Unfortunately, cheetahs are on the endangered species list, and their survival will depend on thoughtful, concerned people around the world.

"The Legend of the Cheetah," a version of a Senegal legend as told by Carole Shelton

The indigenous people of Senegal have a legend about the cheetah.

Once, a long time ago, the people of a small village in Senegal thrived in a fertile valley. The villagers shared a small common field and fifty or more cattle. Traders often stopped at the village as they made their way to the great Senegal River.

One morning, as the villagers made ready for their daily chores, they noticed a lone female cheetah near the village. This caused great concern, for the people feared that she was stalking their cattle or lying in wait for some unsuspecting person. But they also knew that it was strange for a cheetah to venture so close to a village. For you see, cheetahs are well aware of man's cruelty and the senseless slaughter of them and their cubs for their fur.

For more than a month, the cheetah stayed within a stone's throw of the village near an ancient Balboa tree. Day after day the villagers watched and listened as the female cheetah called out. So pitiful were the cheetah's cries that all the villagers felt her loss. They understood what had happened. Traders, who had stopped in their village earlier, had taken the cubs while the mother cheetah was out hunting. The traders knew they could sell the cheetah cubs for a great price.

Weeks passed, and day after day, the mother cheetah called out for her cubs. Her golden spotted coat became lifeless. Thin by nature, the cheetah took on more of a skeleton-like appearance for she would not eat. Tears streamed down her face until black marks appeared around her eyes as she wailed for her cubs.

One morning, as the villagers prepared to work in their fields, they stopped and listened. They did not hear the cheetah's cry. She was not at the Balboa tree. Where was she? As they walked toward the fields, they found the cheetah's lifeless body in the tall grass. She had died of a broken heart from the loss of her cubs.

The villagers were so moved that they wrapped the lifeless body of the cheetah in a burial cloth and buried her near the Balboa tree. They placed large stones upon the grave to protect her body from scavengers. When the villagers finished the grave, they gathered together and asked the Great Spirit of the Balboa tree to bring the cheetah peace in the afterlife and one day unite her again with her cubs.

Today this legend is told among the people of Senegal. From that time forward in honor of the love and perseverance of the mother cheetah, all cheetahs are marked with black stains upon their faces in memory of the tears shed so long ago by one faithful cheetah. This mark is to remind mankind to be fair and responsible in their treatment of all animals.

About the Teller

Carole Shelton is a retired teacher and special education supervisor from St. Louis Public Schools. She holds a master's degree in communication arts from Webster University. Currently she volunteers as a reader for the program "Reading Is Fundamental" (RIF). Contact her by e-mail at cesstoryteller@aol.com.

Telling Tips

This story is realistic until the very end. Factual information about the cheetah is used throughout the story. At the end, the legend explains the black marks on the cheetah's face as the tears shed for her young cubs. It is not repetitive like some folktales. One event follows the other. This story relies heavily upon the teller's skills to use the words, gestures, and facial expressions to connect with the audience.

Story Path

1. A cheetah is seen prowling the outskirts of a village.

2. The people notice her crying and realize that she is sad because the traders have taken her cubs.

3. They hear her crying for days on end but can do nothing to help her.

4. The mother cheetah dies of a broken heart.

5. The villagers bury her and ask that the Great Spirit bring her peace and reunite her with her cubs.

6. Since that day, cheetahs have tear stains on their faces.

Right There

1. Where did the villagers usually see the cheetah?

2. Why is the mother cheetah crying?

Think and Search

1. What information did the storyteller share about cheetahs?

2. What information in the tale is factual, and what information is part of the legend?

Author and Me

1. Why didn't the villagers do more to help the cheetah when they noticed her losing weight?

2. What could have been done to help the mother cheetah?

3. What might have made the traders think that their treatment of the cheetah was fair?

On My Own

1. Do we have an obligation to help endangered animals?

2. Who decides what is fair in the treatment of animals?

3. How could you convince people to be fair in their treatment of animals?

Post-Telling—Looking at Point of View

What might have made the traders think that their treatment of the cheetah was fair?

How do you think the villagers and the mother cheetah would respond to the traders?

Traders' Response	Villagers' Response	Mother Cheetah's Response
Capturing cheetah cubs is how we make a living. Without the cheetah cubs, we can't support our families.		
We didn't hurt the cubs. We sold them to someone. We are not responsible for what happens to them after we sell them.		
The mother cheetah just gave up. She should have gone on with her life and had more cubs.		
The mother cheetah should not have left her cubs unwatched for so long.		
The villagers should have done something to help the cheetah.		
Cheetahs are vicious animals that attack villagers. We were helping the villagers by eliminating an enemy.		

Additional Sources

Books

Hurst, Carol Otis, and Rebecca Otis. *A Killing in Plymouth Colony.* Boston: Houghton Mifflin Harcourt, 2003.

     This is a story about the young John Bradford and his father, Governor William Bradford. John is struggling to build a relationship with his father, who is consumed with his duties as governor. When someone is murdered, a conflict develops between the governor and John.

Rockwell, Anne, and R. Gregory Christie. *Only Passing Through: The Story of Sojourner Truth.* New York: Random House Children's Books, 2002.

     This picture book covers the early years of Sojourner Truth and the unfair treatment she received. It follows her to the time she became an advocate for civil rights.

Web Sites

A United States History Web site about inequality and fairness fighters. Quizzes and activities about fairness: http://pbskids.org/wayback/fair/index.html.

Meeting of the Minds is one way of looking at other points of view. This Web site has an example of the Meeting of the Minds Technique: http://www.readwritethink.org/lessons/lesson_view.asp?id=227.

What's Fair in a Free Country: http://edsitement.neh.gov/view_lesson_plan.asp?id=339.

Honesty

Pre-Telling—On My Own

1. What do we mean when we say a person is honest?

2. Why can it sometimes be difficult to be honest?

3. What do you think this quotation means: "We tell lies when we are afraid . . . afraid of what we don't know, afraid of what others will think, afraid of what will be found out about us. But every time we tell a lie, the thing that we fear grows stronger." —Tad Williams, science fiction author. (You can find this quote at http://quotes.liberty-tree.ca/quote/tad_williams_quote_dbf8 or http://www.brainyquote.com/quotes/authors/t/tad_williams.html.)

Making Predictions about Characters (Predict-A-Character Chart)

Explain to the students that they will be meeting three characters in the next story: An emperor, a young boy, and the young boy's father. If needed, define the word *emperor* for the students. (For example: The leader of our country is called the president. In ancient times, people lived in areas called empires instead of countries. China and Rome were called empires, so the leader of an empire is called an emperor.)

Now tell the students that you are going to give words or phrases that can describe the three characters they will be meeting in the story. Read the first word; have students repeat the word. Ask if anyone can explain the word or provide a definition. Allow a student to define the term and provide additional information as needed. Following each explanation, ask students to connect the word or phrase to one of the three characters, then make a prediction. For example, which character do you think will be a skilled gardener? Why did you select that character? Are you basing your prediction on someone you know or someone you have read about in a different story? Have students explain their choices. Perhaps they know someone who is a skilled gardener; perhaps they have met a character in another book who was a skilled gardener. It is perfectly all right to assign a word to more than one character. (This is an On My Own activity because the students have not yet been introduced to the story. They must use their own schema to make predictions that connect the words to characters.)

Which character will have the following traits or characteristics?

Long white beard	Clever	Honest
Wealthy	Wise	Respectful
Skilled gardener	Good and kind	Persistent

Emperor	Young Boy (Ling)	Boy's Father

"The Emperor's Flowers," a story from China as told by Marilyn Kinsella

Once upon a time there was an emperor of China. He was good and kind—a good leader of his country. Whenever he wasn't busy running his country, he liked to walk through his garden. It was a beautiful garden full of waterfalls, birds, and every kind of flower imaginable. But, one day, as the emperor was walking in his garden, he thought perhaps it was time for him to select someone who, one day, would take his place on the throne. He had no family of his own.

He thought, "How can I select a new emperor . . . someone who is willing to serve the people; someone who is smart and brave; someone who can make the right decision even though it may not be a popular one?" He reached to take a dying flower off the vine, and several seeds fell into his hand. Suddenly, he had an idea.

He wrote a decree that was sent to all the provinces. The decree read, "The emperor is looking for someone to take his place as ruler of the great land of China. The child who can grow the most beautiful plants from the seeds of the royal garden shall take his royal majesty's place."

Ling was a young boy who lived in a far away province. He was a wonderful gardener. It seemed everything he tried to grow flourished. So he asked his father if he could go the palace. His father looked at him. "Son, this is a huge undertaking. You must promise to do your best."

"Oh, yes, father! I will do my VERY best."

So Ling went to the royal palace. He was surprised to see all the other children who were already there. He waited anxiously until the emperor walked out onto the patio of his high window. The emperor was an old man with long white hair braided down his back. His white beard reached to his waist. He wore a silk brocade robe with long full sleeves. Ling and the others bowed low until the emperor spoke.

"My children, I am so happy to see so many of you today. I must choose my successor wisely. That is why I am having a contest. Whoever can take the seeds from the royal garden and grow the most beautiful flowers, will be the next ruler of the great land of China. In six months you are to return with your pots with flowers grown from these seeds. Are you ready?"

The children applauded politely and again bowed their heads.

"Very well! Guards, you may disperse the flower seeds." The guards gave each child a little sack filled with seeds. When Ling received his pouch, he bowed to the guard and thanked him. Then, the children went back to their homes.

Ling was so excited when he got back home. He told his family about the emperor, the palace, and the seeds. His father looked at his son, "I am very proud of you, son. You have taken the first step. Now, it is time to prepare the soil, so you can plant the seeds."

After finding a big pot, Ling prepared the soil. He wondered what kind of plant would grow. Would it be tall or short? Lots of green leaves? Red, yellow, or blue flowers?

Each day he went out to tend the pot making sure it had just enough but not too much water. Each day he anxiously awaited the first sign of the plant peeking through the soil. Each day . . . he waited, and waited . . . and . . . Nothing! Nothing grew. Ling felt panic in his heart. "Father, what can I do?"

"Try putting it into another pot. Perhaps, that will help." But after a few more weeks, the seeds still did not sprout. He tried putting it in the sun and in the shade. Nothing.

The time came for the children to return to the palace. "Father, I will disgrace the family. Nothing grew!"

"Ling, did you do your best?"

"Yes, father, I did."

"Then, you must return to the palace. You have honored your family by trying your best. It won't be easy, but you must finish what you started."

Ling sadly got a cart and put his pot, void of any flowers, into it and started on his journey back to the palace.

As he got closer to the palace gate, he could see other boys proudly bringing their pots filled with gorgeous flowers. When they looked at Ling's empty pot, they began to laugh.

Ling's heart was heavy as he entered the royal garden. He found a place in the back where he hoped the emperor would not see him. This time the emperor came out the door and began walking down the rows of flowers. Every once in a while, he looked at a plant and smiled. Finally, he came to Ling, but the emperor had no smile on his face.

"Who are you and what is this?" he demanded.

Ling's eyes filled with tears, but he held them back as he said, "Your Majesty, my name is Ling. I am honored that you gave me the seeds from the royal garden to grow. I tried my best, but they would not grow. I am sorry, Your Majesty." His head hung in shame.

With that, the emperor walked back into the palace, and seconds later he was at the high window. He looked out at all the children and the plants.

"Today, I have found the child who will one day rule China. There is only one child here who did as I asked—to plant the seeds I gave you. I do not know where the rest of you found the seeds to grow such beautiful plants, but it was not from the royal garden. For, you see, I had the gardeners bake the seeds until they would not grow. Only one child among you came with truth, honesty, perseverance, and integrity growing in his pot, and that young man, the next emperor of China is . . . Ling.

Ling looked up in surprise as he saw the emperor smiling and gesturing toward him.

And so it was that Ling and his family came to live at the palace. When he was old enough and educated, he became the emperor of China. They say that he ruled well and that China prospered just like the flowers he grew in the royal garden.

Telling Tips

The characters in this story are Chinese, but it is best to tell the story in your natural voice rather than try to create an accent that might be offensive or inaccurate. It is easy to add actions to this story. For example, pretend to be the emperor reaching out to the dead flowers on the vine. Pretend to be reading from a scroll as the decree is being read.

Story Path

1. The emperor is a good and kind man who loves his royal garden.

2. While walking in his garden, he devises a plan to select the next emperor.

3. He sends out a decree explaining how the next emperor will be chosen.

4. Ling asks his father if he can go to the palace, and his father agrees.

5. All of the children receive their flower seeds from the guards.

6. Ling returns home to plant his seeds, but they do not grow.

7. He asks his father for advice.

8. After several weeks, it is time to return to the palace.

9. Ling is ashamed of his empty pot, but his father convinces him that he must finish what he started and that he should not be ashamed because he tried his best.

10. Ling stands with the other children as the emperor walks among them.

11. The emperor asks Ling his name, and Ling tearfully answers.

12. The emperor announces that Ling will be the next emperor.

Right There

1. Where did Ling live?

2. What response does Ling's father give when Ling asks permission to go to the palace?

3. What is the first thing Ling does when he returns home from his trip to the palace?

4. Where was the emperor walking when he devised his plan to select the next emperor?

Think and Search

1. Please list all of the things that Ling did to help his flowers grow.

2. Sit eye-to-eye, knee-to-knee with a partner and recreate the conversation between Ling and his father for the following scenes:

    Ling asking permission to go to the palace to get flower seeds

    Ling asking his father for advice when the plants are not growing

    Ling talking with his father right before he takes his empty pot to the palace

    Ling explaining his failure to the emperor

Author and Me

1. Describe the relationship between Ling and his father.

2. What kind of things did Ling learn from his father?

3. What kind of character traits do you think Ling learned from his father?

4. How did Ling learn these character traits?

5. Do you think that Ling's father was proud of his son?

Post-Telling

- Return to the Predict-A-Character Chart

- Which predictions were correct, and which ones must be changed? Use the instructional vocabulary of QAR. For example, the words *good* and *kind* can be placed under the emperor column because the information is Right There in the story. The words *good* and *kind* can also be placed under the father, but students must make an inference to draw that conclusion. What happened in the text that lets us infer that the father is good and kind? What did the author have the father say or do to prove that he is good and kind?

Freeze Frames

Scene 1: The emperor explains the contest as the children listen.

Scene 2: Ling asks his father for advice when his plant is not growing.

Scene 3: Ling brings his empty pot to the palace, and the other boys laugh.

Scene 4: The emperor announces Ling as his successor.

Post-Reading Graphic Organizer for Author and Me Work

Prompt: Was Ling's father truly proud of his son?		
Story Says	**My Ideas**	**Help Others to See and Understand Your Ideas**
Words from the text	Explain what those words mean to you	Use any of these techniques to help the reader understand your ideas: compare and contrast • analyze word choice, symbols, or literary devices • make connections • visualize • infer and imply • draw a conclusion
The father says, "Then, you must return to the palace. You have honored your family by trying your best. It won't be easy, but you must finish what you started."	The father says that Ling has honored the family. Because he encourages Ling to go back to the palace, it proves that he is proud of his son. If he felt embarrassed, he would have let his son hide at home.	I can visualize the father looking into his son's eyes and maybe putting his arm on his son's shoulder. His steady gaze and physical closeness to his son proves that he is proud. If he were ashamed, he would look away and stammer with his answer. At no time does the father doubt his son or feel ashamed of his efforts.

Additional Sources

Books

Demi. *The Empty Pot*. New York: Henry Holt, 1996.

Numerous versions of this story exist, and each has a different name for the boy. In the version we have given you, the young boy is called Ling. In *The Empty Pot,* the young boy is named Ping. *The Empty Pot* is beautifully told by Demi and also features amazing illustrations. A careful study of the illustrations and the interesting use of colors will help students to understand Ping's thoughtful nature.

Lowry, Lois. *Your Move, J.P.!* Boston: Houghton Mifflin Harcourt, 1990.

J.P. Tate has fallen in love with Angela Patricia Galsworthy. To impress her, he concocts a lie that he has a fatal disease. His lie becomes a major problem because Angela's father is a specialist in genetic disorders. J.P. must now squirm his way out of his lies.

Respect

Pre-Telling—On My Own

Complete the following statements:

1. When people make fun of me, I feel . . .

2. When I make fun of others, I feel . . .

3. I know that people respect me when . . .

4. It is important to me to have the respect of . . .

"Phaeton and Apollo," a Greek myth as told by Phyllis Hostmeyer

In the time when Greek gods ruled, Apollo, the Sun god was in charge of escorting the sun across the sky. Apollo lived on Mount Olympus with the other Greek gods, and every day he served humankind. Unfortunately, children could not live on Mount Olympus, so Phaeton lived on earth with his mother Clymene.

One day at school, Phaeton bragged to his classmates. "My father is Apollo, the Sun god. Every day he drives the chariot of fire across the sky to bring warmth and light to our days."

Phaeton's classmates laughed and ridiculed him. They did not believe a word he said. For days on end, they hurled insults at Phaeton and accused him of making up a ridiculous story. They taunted him, "If Apollo is your father, prove it. Ask him to let you drive the chariot of fire across the sky. Only when we see you at the reins will we believe that you are his son."

In a rage, Phaeton approached his mother. "You claim that Apollo is my father, and yet he has never visited, has never played games, or laughed with me. If Apollo really is my father, please give me the proof I need so that I can make my classmates stop laughing. Give me proof that will help me to earn their respect."

Clymene saw the hurt and confusion in her son's face. With that, she said, "Phaeton, your father is indeed Apollo, and he loves you. But you know it is his task to drive the team of horses that pull the chariot of fire across the sky each day. He cannot leave his post, but you, my son, can go to meet your father."

And that night Phaeton left his home and journeyed east to find his father. Once he reached the land of the sunrise, he saw his father's home. The palace of the sun stood aloft in the clouds; it was covered with gold and precious stones. Phaeton walked up the marble steps, through the silver doors, and entered the halls of his father's palace. He followed the long hall until he came to the throne room where he saw his father sitting upon a diamond-encrusted throne. He wore a crown of sunbeams, and Phaeton stopped at a distance because the light was too much for his eyes to bear.

When Apollo saw his son, he called out to him, "Phaeton, my son, why have you traveled such a distance? Does your mother know that you are here?"

"Mother has allowed me to come so that I can gather proof that you are indeed my father. My classmates torment me and laugh at me every day."

Apollo removed his crown of beams and stepped down from the throne. He held out his arms, and Phaeton rushed to his embrace. "My son, ask for anything and it will be yours. I will give you whatever proof you need to hush the boys that mock you."

Without hesitation, Phaeton said, "Let me drive the horses and chariot across the sky so that my classmates on Earth can see me at the reins. That will prove you are my father."

Apollo shook his head. "Phaeton, you do not know what you are asking. You are too young and small to control the team of horses. Not even Zeus, whose powerful arm hurls the lightning bolts, has the strength to handle the chariot. The first part of the trip is so steep that the horses struggle until they reach the top. The middle part of the trip is so high in the heavens that even I shudder when I look down and see the earth and the oceans stretched out beneath me. The last part of the trip heads downward in a path so steep that Tethys, who brings the horses back to the stables each night, trembles with the fear that I might fall from the chariot. Please ask for something else."

But Phaeton shook his head and replied, "Father, the only thing that will end the ridicule is for my classmates to see me driving the chariot of fire across the sky."

"Phaeton, you don't understand the danger of this trip. There isn't a clear path for you to follow; instead, you must steer the chariot through the middle of frightful monsters that live in the sky. You must pass the horns of the bull and the jaws of the lion. The Scorpion stretches its arms in one direction and the Crab in another. And all the while the heaven is spinning 'round and 'round carrying the stars along their paths. Your request is foolish and will surely bring you death. Please, I beg you, ask for anything else and it is yours."

Phaeton crossed his arms and stared at his father. He stood firm in his demand. Apollo's heart was heavy with grief, for he had no choice but to grant the wish. Once the oath is sworn, it cannot be changed. Having done all he could to dissuade his son, he finally led Phaeton to the stables and hooked up the fire-breathing horses to the chariot. He then rubbed magic oil on Phaeton's skin to protect him from the heat. He set the crown of rays upon Phaeton's head and said, "A few words of advice. Hold the reins tight and do not whip the horses. They will go fast enough of their own accord. You will see the tracks from past trips; try to stay on that path. Don't let the horses run too high or you will scorch the heavens and leave the Earth cold. And do not let them run too low or you will set the earth aflame."

With that Phaeton sprang into the chariot, stood tall, and grasped the reins. The air rang with the snorts and fiery breath of the horses that stamped the ground. Rosy-fingered Dawn threw open the stable doors, and the Moon prepared to retire. The horses, seeing the boundless stretch of universe in front of them, leaped forward to begin their daily trip. Soon they realized that the hand that held the rein lacked the strength to hold them. They lurched forward with blazing speed. When Phaeton saw the earth grow small beneath him, he grew pale and his legs trembled.

Desperate to slow the team of horses, Phaeton pulled hard on the reins, but the horses raced high into the sky and left the Earth extremely dark and cold. Phaeton saw the monstrous forms scattered across the sky. The crooked claws of the Scorpion and his two great arms seemed to lurch toward the boy. He cowered on the floor of the chariot and covered his eyes. His screams pierced the air. Apollo could hear the frightened cries of the people on Earth who had been thrown into a freezing darkness without warning. He screamed to Phaeton, "Turn the horses around." Hearing his father's voice, the boy stood up and made a desperate attempt to change course.

In the next second, the horses made a path straight down. Phaeton saw the tracks of yesterday's trip and used all his weight to pull the reins to the right and get the horses onto that path. But they continued their rapid descent and came so close to Earth that lakes and rivers dried up. Great cities perished as their walls and towers crumbled beneath the heat. People turned to ash. Phaeton now realized that his father had been right, and he wished that he had listened.

Zeus roared at Apollo, "What foolishness is this? Your son will destroy all of Earth and the heavens too, if he is not stopped."

"I promised him anything not knowing he would ask to drive the chariot. There was nothing I could do to stop him. You know as well as I that once we make a promise, the oath must be fulfilled no matter what the consequence. What would you have me do?"

As plants withered and entire forests burned, Zeus realized he must do something to stop the total destruction of Earth. "Apollo, turn your eyes away from the boy. You have left me no choice."

Zeus selected the smallest of his lightning bolts and launched it toward the chariot. It struck Phaeton and knocked him from the chariot. He tumbled through the skies like a falling star and landed into the water below.

The horses, growing weary, returned to the stables. But for many, many days, Apollo would not drive the chariot. Weeping, he wandered along the banks of the river where his son had fallen. Even the poplar trees lamented the boy and cried tears of amber for Phaeton. Eventually the pleas of the people on Earth, left in darkness and cold, persuaded Apollo to return to his daily task of driving the chariot of fire across the sky.

Telling Tips

Pause after saying these lines, "Phaeton crossed his arms and stared at his father. He stood firm in his demand." Stop at this point and ask the students what they think Apollo should do. Take a few of their ideas and then explain to them that once Greek gods made a promise, they had to fulfill it. Because Apollo cannot convince his son to ask for something else, he must allow the child to drive the chariot.

Story Path

1. Phaeton lives on Earth with his mother Clymene.

2. Phaeton brags to his classmates that Apollo is his father, and his classmates ridicule him.

3. Phaeton demands proof from his mother, who then gives him permission to travel to his father's palace.

4. Apollo greets his son, listens to his problem, and then promises him anything.

5. Phaeton asks to drive the chariot.

6. Apollo tries to discourage his son by explaining that not even Zeus has the power to handle the chariot. He tells him the path is steep and dangerous.

7. Phaeton stands firm in his demand.

8. Apollo again explains the danger: there is no clear path, the sky is filled with monsters, the heavens spin nonstop.

9. Phaeton still stands firm in his demand.

10. Apollo, left no choice but to grant the wish, takes his son to the stables and gives him three things: protective oil, the crown of rays, and words of advice.

11. Phaeton jumps into the chariot, and the horses, realizing a stranger is driving, ascend high into the heavens.

12. Seeing the monsters in the sky, Phaeton cowers in the chariot until his father calls to him.

13. Phaeton struggles to turn the horses around, but they begin to plunge toward Earth, destroying cities, rivers, and people.

14. Zeus screams at Apollo who says he had no choice in the matter.

15. Zeus tells Apollo to turn his eyes away, and he throws a lightning bolt at Phaeton.

16. Phaeton falls from the chariot, and the horses return.

17. Apollo mourns for days until the cries of the people on Earth persuade him to return to driving the chariot across the skies.

Right There

1. Who is Phaeton's father?

2. Why is Phaeton angry when he returns home from school?

3. What proof of heritage do his classmates demand from Phaeton?

4. What does Phaeton's mother give him permission to do?

Think and Search

1. What behaviors does Phaeton display at school and at home before he is given permission to visit his father?

2. Sit with a partner and recreate the scene between Phaeton and his father when Phaeton has asked permission to drive the chariot.

Author and Me

1. What lines in the story might infer that Phaeton doubts his father's love?

2. How do you visualize Apollo's body language when he is trying to persuade Phaeton to ask for something different? How does his body language convey his feelings at the time?

3. Why do you think Phaeton bragged to his classmates about his father?

4. Do you think that Phaeton's classmates had a right to ridicule him?

5. Why was it so important to Phaeton that he earn the respect of his classmates?

6. Why do you think Phaeton would not listen to his father's warnings?

7. Phaeton was certain that driving the chariot would help him win his classmates' respect. What could he have done instead to earn that respect?

Post-Telling—*Why Did You Do It* Poem

Why Did You Do It? Sample:

Question / Prompt	Response
Why did you do it?	I had always dreamed of pulling the chariot across the sky.
Why did you do it?	I had always dreamed of being like my father.
Describe the weather.	The crystal sun heated my pale skin.
Was anyone else there?	The stallions raced when they noticed the unfamiliar hand at the reins.
Was anyone else there?	Frightened, the people watched their world turn to ash.
Why did you do it?	I did it to stop the laughter of my classmates.
Why did you do it?	I did it because my father made me a promise.
Why did you do it?	I did it to show everyone that my father is Apollo, and I am Phaeton—his son.

Additional Sources

Books

Hamilton, Edith. *Mythology.* New York: Little, Brown & Company, 1998.
   Hamilton's tellings of the Greek myths have become a classic resource for those interested in learning more about Greek mythology.

Yolen, Jane, and Robert Harris. *Girl in a Cage.* New York: Penguin Group, 2004.
   Marjorie, the daughter of a Scottish king, is imprisoned in a cage. She maintains her self-respect in spite of abuse, ridicule, and horrible living conditions.

Responsibility

Pre-Telling—On My Own

1. Are there ever times that you have been irresponsible?

2. What are the consequences of irresponsible behavior?

3. What are the consequences of always making excuses for irresponsible behavior?

We all know that one way to show responsibility is to listen respectfully to our parents, guardians, teachers, and others. Responsible people consider the advice and rules they have been given and work hard to obey. But sometimes, for whatever reason, people don't follow the rules and advice. What are some reasons we sometimes fail to act responsibly, or why do we sometimes break rules or stray from good advice?

Are any of these reasons a good excuse for irresponsible behavior?

The following story is about a young boy who forgot to follow some good advice.

"Daedalus and Icarus," a Greek myth as told by Phyllis Hostmeyer

Daedalus was known throughout the land for his genius as an inventor; he was a solver of problems. King Minos commanded Daedalus to build the labyrinth, an enormous maze with numberless winding passages and turns that opened one into the other. The Minotaur, a monstrous creature half-bull and half-man, was to live inside the labyrinth on the island of Crete. Minos built a maze so complicated that it seemed to have no beginning or end. This made King Minos happy.

Unfortunately, the day came that Daedalus fell into disfavor with King Minos. In anger, he locked Daedalus and his son Icarus into a tower and refused to let them leave the island. Knowing that the crafty Daedalus might find a way to escape the tower, King Minos assigned many guards to keep a strict watch on all ships and would not allow any of them to sail away from the island without first being thoroughly searched.

"Minos may control the land and sea," said Daedalus, "but he has no control over the air. We will make our escape that way." Daedalus spent many days watching the birds that flew overhead. He studied the shape of their wings and the way the feathers overlapped. Using this knowledge, he began building wings for himself and Icarus. He tied the feathers together, beginning with the smallest and adding larger ones, so as to form an increasing surface. He secured the feathers with wax and shaped the wings into a gentle curvature like the wings of a bird.

Icarus watched his father work and would often run to gather up the feathers blowing in the wind. He loved playing with the wax and working it with his fingers. His father laughed at the boy's curiosity even though his playing often interfered with the work of building the wings.

When the last feather was in place, Daedalus tested the wings. He was thrilled when he found he could rise into the air, hang suspended, or move left and right with slight movements. Then, as a bird leads her babies from a lofty nest, he taught young Icarus how to fly. He cautioned his son, "Do not fly too close to the water, which will dampen your wings and clog the feathers, making it difficult to fly. Even more important, do not fly too high, or the heat of the sun will melt the wax. Stay close to me, and you will be safe." To assure himself that his son had listened, he made his son repeat his advice.

The following day, he fit the wings to his son's shoulders. Tears lined the father's face, and his hands trembled as he fastened the straps that held the wings tight. He kissed his son and once more repeated his warning, "Remember, Icarus, stay near me. Do not go near the water. And please stay away from the sun, or its heat will melt the wax." Then flapping his wings, Daedalus rose into the sky and called for his son to follow. As they flew, farmers stopped their work and pointed skyward. Astonished at the sight of men dancing on air, shepherds leaned on their staffs and watched these human birds.

Father and son passed the islands of Samos and Delos and stayed on the course to freedom. But soon Icarus grew bored with following his father. He began to try trick moves, flipping head over heel, soaring left and then veering right. Thrilled with the joy of flying, Icarus forgot his father's words, and he began to soar upward as if he meant to reach the heavens. He closed his eyes, and with a mighty thrust of his wings, he powered himself higher and higher. He languished for a few seconds, enjoying the sense of floating on a draft of air.

Daedalus saw Icarus rising above him and called to him, "Icarus, stop, turn back." But the boy had flown too high to hear his father. Daedalus used all of his strength to flap his wings in an attempt to reach his son. As he fought his way through the air, he saw feathers floating by. Again he called, "Icarus, come back. You are too close to the sun. Come back, Icarus!"

The blazing sun melted the wax, and one by one the feathers fell from the framework. Icarus felt himself falling and fluttered his wings in a desperate attempt to stay aloft, but there were no feathers left to support him. He screamed, "Father, help! Save me!" His body plunged downward as his father watched helplessly. Icarus fell into the South Sea of Samos.

Daedalus screamed, "My skills have killed my only son. I wish we had stayed prisoners on Crete where at least my son would be alive." Consumed with grief, Daedalus forced himself to continue his flight. Eventually, he made his way to Sicily, where he grieved the loss of his son. Eventually, the Sea of Samos became known as the Icarian Sea in memory of a young boy who forgot his father's advice.

Telling Tips

Because the bulk of this story revolves around only two characters, it is an easy story for students to follow. Nonetheless, a slight shift in voice when Daedalus is speaking can help students to visualize the father and to understand his range of emotions. Decide how you will make Daedalus sound confident and thoughtful when he decides that the king cannot control the skies. Demonstrate that he is patient but obviously worried when he explains to Icarus the importance of staying close. Use your voice and body to show the father's terror when he calls to his son to come back. Let your listeners hear and see that Daedalus is consumed with grief by the end of the story.

Story Path

1. Introduction of Daedalus and his skills in building the labyrinth.

2. Daedalus falls out of favor with King Minos and is imprisoned with his son.

3. King Minos patrols the sea and land, so Daedalus decides to fly to freedom.

4. Daedalus studies the birds, and he and his son build the wings.

5. Daedalus tests the wings.

6. Daedalus cautions his son.

7. Daedalus and his son fly to freedom.

8. Icarus becomes enchanted with flight and forgets his father's warnings.

9. Icarus comes too close to the sun, which melts the wax.

10. Daedalus tries to save his son but is too late.

11. Daedalus grieves his son but must fly on.

Right There

1. What did Daedalus build for King Minos?

2. Why are Daedalus and Icarus imprisoned?

3. Why can't they escape from the island by sea?

Think and Search

Make a list of the interactions between Daedalus and his son from the beginning of the story until they take flight.

Author and Me

1. How would you describe the relationship between Daedalus and his son?

2. Why do you think Icarus did not follow the advice of his father?

3. Was Icarus a responsible child?

Post-Telling

Following the discussion, ask why we sometimes do not follow rules and advice.

Discussion

Brainstorm some examples of irresponsible behavior; then determine the consequences. For example:

Irresponsible Behavior	Consequence of Irresponsible Behavior
Not doing homework	
Littering	
Yelling and slamming doors if I don't get my way.	

Poetry

Create an *I Am* poem. Answer as though you are Daedalus or Icarus.

Additional Sources

Books

Giff, Patricia Reilly. *Nory Ryan's Song.* New York: Random House Children's Books, 2002.

This historical fiction piece tells the story of twelve-year-old Nory Ryan and the problems that beset her family during the Great Famine in Ireland between 1845 and 1852. People are hungry, and food sources are disappearing rapidly. Nory takes on immense responsibilities to help her family and her community survive the famine.

Rawls, Wilson. *Where the Red Fern Grows.* New York: Random House Children's Books, 1961.

This classic story introduces students to Billy and his coonhounds. Billy takes responsibility for his dogs and is also a responsible hunter. When tragedy strikes, Billy learns the Native American legend of the sacred red fern.

Web Sites

Lesson plans on responsible behavior and not making excuses: http://curriculalessons. suite101.com/article.cfm/lesson_plan_taking_responsibility.

Lesson plans on responsible pet care: http://www.kindnews.org/teacher_zone/lesson_ plans.asp.

This Web site provides lesson plans on how human activities have affected the Chesapeake Watershed. It deals with environmental responsibility: http://www.nationalgeographic. com/xpeditions/lessons/14/g35.

Music

Dayton Philharmonic Orchestra, "Inventing Flight: Daedalus and Icarus," on the album *A Celebration of Flight* (available as an MP3 download on Amazon.com)

USAF Concert Band, "First Flight: Daedalus and Icarus," from the album *Born of Dreams: First Flights* (available as an MP3 download on Amazon.com)

Chapter 6

Stories, QARs, and Activities for Grades 7 and 8

See Chapter 3 for instructions and samples of all activities.

Caring

Pre-Telling—On My Own

1. Do you know any ways that we can help people in need?

2. Are there any special times when people help others more than usual?

3. Are there times when it might be okay to say no when someone needs help?

4. What are some synonyms for caring? What are some antonyms for caring?

5. Why do we give help to those who are in need?

6. What professions might you consider working in, if you are a person who likes to care for others?

7. Have you ever known anyone who did something wrong, and then others never wanted to have anything to do with him or her again? How do you think that feels?

8. Have you ever known anyone who did something wrong, and others did give them a chance to prove they were worthy? How do you think it feels to have a second chance?

Walk and Gawk

Assign students to one of the charts that has a question about Caring from the "Smorgasbord of Activities" in Chapter 3. Students brainstorm ideas as an On My Own activity and return to it after hearing and discussing the story.

"Woodpecker Song," a nature myth from the Native American Woodland Peoples as told by Lynn Rubright

Introduction: Long ago some people believed the Great Spirit could change himself into many forms. He could become a rock, an animal, or even a man. Now and again, some legends say, he would turn himself into a man and walk the earth to test the hearts of men and women to see if they were kind and good or cruel and evil.

Once there was a woman who lived alone in a small lodge next to a great wood. One day, dressed in a long black skirt with a red shawl over her head and shoulders, she prepared her food by grinding corn. Mixing the meal with a little water, she patted it into a corn cake and placed it on her hot baking stone.

When she heard a twig snap behind her, she was surprised to see an old man slowly walk out of the deep woods. His wrinkled skin hung loose on his bones. His matted grey hair hung in two braids over his stooped shoulders. In a crackling voice he said to her, "I have traveled many moons in the dark forest eating nothing but berries from bushes and insects from the barks of trees. Do you have something to give me to eat? I am very hungry."

The woman took pity on the old man and said, "I have a corn cake baking. Why not rest yourself against that tree, and I will call you when it is done."

The old man knelt against the tree, crossed his arms over his chest, and seemed to fall asleep while he waited.

When the corn cake was done, the woman pulled it off the baking stone and held it in the folds of her long black skirt. But she was puzzled. It seemed much larger than the one she had placed on the stone to bake. She glanced at the old man. He still seemed to be asleep. Instead of waking him, she entered her lodge and hid the corn cake under furs lying on the ground.

When she came out, she saw the old man looking at her. "Is the corn cake done yet?" he asked.

The woman lied, "That corn cake burned. Rest yourself a while longer while I bake another one."

The old man replied, "I will wait," and again he seemed to doze.

This time the woman crushed fewer corn kernels than before on her grinding stones and made a corn cake smaller than the first one. Adding twigs to the fire, she watched and waited while it baked. She noticed the corn cake growing larger. When it was done, she picked it up and held it in her long skirt. It was much larger than the first one she had baked. She wondered, "Do I have magic corn, a magic baking stone, or magic hands?" Glancing at the man to be sure he was still asleep, the woman hurried into her lodge and hid that corn cake with the first one she had baked.

Again the old man was awake when she came out of her lodge. "Is the corn cake done yet?" he asked.

The woman lied again. "That corn cake fell into the ashes. Rest yourself a while longer and I will make you yet another."

The old man said, "I will wait," and he closed his eyes.

This time the woman took only two small corn kernels and ground them into a pinch of meal. She added only a few drops of water making a tiny corn cake that she then placed on the baking stone. She watched and waited.

Her heart filled with joy as the corn cake grew larger and larger. When it was done, she held the great corn cake in her long skirt and twirled around thinking, "I do have magic corn, or a magic stone, or magic hands! I will take this great corn cake to a tribal feast and my people will bow down before me, for I have magic powers." Then she remembered the old man. He was still sleeping. The woman hurried into her lodge and hid the great corn cake under the furs with the others.

When she came out of the lodge, the old man was no longer sleeping. He was standing before her. He was no longer old and bent with skin hanging loosely on his bones. He stood tall, and straight, and strong. His smooth skin was brown and firm. His long braids, black and shining as a blackbird's wing, hung over his shoulders. His black eyes glistened as he said sternly, "Woman, where is my corn cake?"

Backing away from him, she said, "I do not know you. You are a stranger. Go back into the woods from where you have come, where you can eat berries from bushes and insects from the bark of trees. I have nothing to give you."

The man clapped his hands loudly. He said, "Woman, from this day forth, *you* will be the one who will eat berries from bushes and insects from the bark of trees."

The woman looked down. Her legs had become the thin little legs of a bird. Her feet had become claws. She saw black feathers growing from her long black skirt. Her arms had become two black wings. Red feathers grew from the red shawl covering her head and neck. Her eyes had become beady little eyes, and her nose had become a beak.

The man clapped his hands again. The woman, now a black bird with the red head, arched her wings and flew to a nearby tree and began pecking for the insects that lived there.

That woman's children and the children's children live in the woods today eating berries from bushes and pecking for insects from the bark of trees. Look and listen. They are the red-headed woodpeckers you can hear and see to this day.

About the Teller

Lynn Rubright is a recipient of the National Storytelling Network's Circle of Excellence Award (1996) and Lifetime Achievement ORACLE Award (2007). She taught Storytelling across the Curriculum for Webster University for thirty-six years, received an Emmy as coproducer of the documentary *Oh Freedom after While*. Her books include *Beyond the Beanstalk: Interdisciplinary Learning through Storytelling* (Heinemann 1996) and *Mama's Window* (Lee and Low Books).

Telling Tips

This story is a cautionary tale that warns what can happen to those who are not kind to the less fortunate. This is an excellent tale for using body language to help children infer what is happening. At the beginning of the tale, hunch over and convey a sense of tiredness when speaking as the old man. Use a weak, gravelly voice. When the woman decides to hide her corn cakes from the sleeping man, convey the dishonesty by glancing about and shifting your eyes to and fro. Take time to show how she hides the corn cakes in the folds of her skirt. Let your face convey her desire for power when she realizes something magical is happening. Slow down at the turning point of the story, and use your voice and body to demonstrate what has happened.

Show the woman's fear of the man who is now strong and tall by backing away as you speak, but also show her contempt for the stranger by spitting out these words: "I do not know you. You are a stranger. Go back into the woods from where you have come, where you can eat berries from bushes and insects from the bark of trees. I have nothing to give you."

Now show the man's power by rising tall and by clapping your hands loudly. When speaking the following lines, emphasize the word *you* by pointing at the woman and raising your voice. "Woman, from this day forth *you* will be the one who will eat berries from bushes and insects from the bark of trees."

Story Path

Like so many fairy tales and myths, this story relies on events happening in sets of three.

1. The old woman meets the man and agrees to provide a meal.

2. Three times she bakes the corn cake; three times it grows large; three times she hides the cake and lies to the man.

3. Only after she hides the third cake is the stranger's true identity revealed.

4. She has been given ample opportunities to show that she cares for the less fortunate but has chosen to lie and deny help.

5. For that she will be punished by being turned into a woodpecker.

Right There

1. What was the old woman doing at the opening of the story?

2. Where had the stranger been prior to approaching the woman?

3. What did the stranger do each time the woman was preparing the corn cakes?

Think and Search

1. What facts did the storyteller give us about the woman?

2. What lies did the woman tell to the stranger?

3. How did she change each corn cake that she baked?

Author and Me

1. Why didn't the woman share one of the corn cakes with the stranger?

2. The story tells us that the woman's heart filled with joy right before she spoke these words: "I do have magic corn, or a magic stone, or magic hands! I will take this great corn cake to a tribal feast and my people will bow down before me, for I have magic powers." What is making her so joyous? How do you think she plans to use her magic powers?

Post-Telling

Return to the Walk and Gawk chart papers to add new ideas.

Story Impressions

Give students the following list of words and have them retell the story in small groups:

woman	woods	corn	man	hungry	rest
baking	puzzled	hid	lied	burned	rest
fewer	kernels	baked	puzzled	magic?	hid
lied	ashes	rest	two kernels	waited	joy
hid	powers	man	strong	eat insects	clapped
you	beak	children	woodpecker		

Additional Sources

Books

Yolen, Jane. *Greyling*. New York: Penguin Group, 1991.

Jane Yolen tells a tale of a selchie, a seal who takes on human form. A fisherman brings home the stray seal pup to his wife, only to discover it has become a beautiful child. They choose to raise the child. One morning, the father is caught at sea in a terrible storm, and only Greyling can save him.

Yolen, Jane, and Floyd Cooper. *Miz Berlin Walks*. New York: Penguin Books, 1997.

A young African American girl and Miz Berlin, an elderly white woman, develop a friendship during evening walks filled with storytelling. It is a beautiful story of two people of different generations and backgrounds who develop a strong caring relationship.

Web Sites

Lesson plans on caring for a pet and being responsible for a pet: http://www.kindnews. org/teacher_zone/lesson_plans.asp.

The origins of this story come from several sources. A version can be found in *Walk in Peace; Legends and Stories of the Michigan Indians* by Simon Otto, an Anishinabe teller (Michigan Indian Press Grand Rapids Inter Tribal Council, 1990). In this version, the mystical figure was Nanaboozhoo. However, there are similar stories with St. Peter as the man who came from the woods. These legends come from Scandinavia. This link is a poem that was written using the elements of that version: http://www.foundationwebsite.org/TheLegendOf TheWoodpecker.pdf.

Citizenship

Pre-Telling—On My Own

1. Are there ever times that you have an opportunity to demonstrate that you are a good citizen?

2. What are some things someone might do that would make others draw the conclusion that the person is not a good citizen?

Walk and Gawk

Assign students to one of the charts that has a question about Citizenship. Students brainstorm ideas as an On My Own activity and return to it after the discussion as an Author and Me activity.

"Kanu Above and Kanu Below," an African tale as told by Marilyn Kinsella

A Story, A Story . . . Let it come . . . let it go.

Once, long ago, the Limba people of Sierra Leone told stories about Kanu Above and Kanu Below. Kanu Above was a great chief who lived and ruled in the sky. Kanu Below was also a great chief. He ruled everything on earth. Kanu Above had everything he ever wanted except for one thing . . . Kanu Below's beautiful daughter. So one day he came down from the heavens and took the chief's daughter to live in the sky.

Kanu Below was so distraught at the loss of his daughter that he could not eat, he could not sleep . . . he could not rule his people. Villagers came to him with their problems, but he could do nothing. Finally, one day, his four under chiefs came to him and said, "We are having many problems in our villages. Strangers have come into our midst."

The first under chief said, "Here is the pest that comes into our village. His name is Spider."

"What does this Spider do that is so bad?" asked the chief.

"Why, he is always spinning his annoying threads—across doorways, between the trees, along the grass. Everywhere the villagers walk, they are covered in sticky webs. They do not like it, and they want Spider out of their village."

Kanu looked down at Spider, "Is it true that you have been spinning your webs where people walk, causing them to trip and fall?"

Spider nodded his head in agreement. "I am sorry. I was only trying to catch bugs for my meals. I will try to do better."

The chief said, "Spider does some troublesome things, but I see much good in this Spider, and I say that the people should give him another chance to show that he is a worthy citizen of the village."

And it was so.

The next under chief said, "Kanu, you won't believe what has invaded my village . . . look . . . a rat! He has sharp teeth and is always gnawing, gnawing, gnawing away. He makes holes in our homes and then steals our rice, our meat, and even our kola nuts! We want him out."

"Rat," said Kanu, "is this true?"

"Yes, Kanu Below, it is true. But, I only take one thing from each house. I take only what my family and I need to live."

The chief said, "Rat, you must promise not to steal from others. Your village will see to it that your family is fed." Then, to the people he said, "I see much good in Rat, and I say that the people should give him another chance to show that he is a worthy citizen of the village."

And it was so.

Then, the next under chief spoke, "Kanu, all this about Spider and Rat, it is nothing compared to this plague on our village. I bring you Anteater. He digs and he digs holes all over the place. My people have fallen and hurt themselves. Anteater is a danger to my village and, whew, he smells terrible."

The chief had to agree. Anteater did smell! Fanning himself he said, "Anteater, is it true that you have been digging holes where people walk?"

"Yes, it is true, but only because I am looking for ants to eat."

"Well, Anteater, I think you can dig for ants that are not along the path. That way the people will not get hurt. And, you must promise to take a bath and get rid of the terrible smell!"

"Yes, Kanu Below, I will do better."

Kanu looked at the villagers and said, "I know that Anteater has caused you problems, but he has promised to do better, and I see much good in him. I say that Anteater can stay and prove that he is a good citizen.

And it was so.

Finally, the last under chief spoke. "Kanu, others have had their problems and mine may seem small compared to them, but it is nonetheless causing great strife amongst my village people."

"Pray tell, what can it be?"

"Look, it is a fly . . . a small, pesky, irritating fly that is always buzzing, buzzing around our heads and biting and stinging."

Kanu looked severely at the Fly. "Can this be true?"

"Oh, yes, Kanu. I often try to find places to land after flying. My wings hurt. When I land on the people, they swat me away and sometimes I do bite them."

"I see. Well, biting and stinging will never make you popular amongst the villagers. You must stop at once."

"Yes, Kanu, I will do better."

Kanu spoke, "See here, this fly has been a pest, but he promises to do better. I see much good in him, and I say he can stay to prove his worth to his community."

And it was so.

As the days passed, Kanu Below became more and more saddened at the loss of his daughter. He called all the villagers together. "My good people, you know my heart is heavy. Kanu Above has taken my daughter to call his own. Is there anyone brave enough to go and try to bring her back?"

The villagers looked at one another in shock. Their eyes said it all. Kanu Above was nothing like their beloved chief. Why, Kanu Above was ruthless! A small mumbling and grumbling rippled through the crowd until one small voice spoke up.

"Kanu Below, you were the only one who believed in me." It was Spider. "Now, I want to help you. I will weave a web up to the sky and find Kanu Above."

Just then, three other voices joined in. "Me too." It was Rat, Anteater, and Fly. "We want to help."

So Spider wove his web and hitched it onto a cloud. When the four reached the sky, they called out "Kanu Above, we need to talk to you!"

Just then, Kanu Above appeared. He looked fierce in his golden robes. "What are you doing here?" he bellowed.

Spider spoke, "We have come to ask you to release Kanu Below's daughter. He misses her greatly."

Kanu Above glared at them, but said, "I see. Well then, we must sit down and eat first. Come."

He led them to a large table. As they sat down, Fly noticed that Kanu whispered something into a servant's ear. After she left, Kanu's eyes shifted back and forth. So Fly followed the servant into the kitchen where he saw her place some strange herb onto the meat. He buzzed back to his friends saying, "Do not eat the meat! Do not eat the meat!"

When the meat was served, Spider said, "Oh, this looks delicious! But in my country below, it is considered a great taboo to eat meat at someone's home, but we will gladly eat the rice with palm oil sauce." And they did.

Kanu Above was angry, but he did not let it show. "Come, my new friends, it is getting late." He showed them to a hut. The minute they got inside, Kanu Above ordered the doors and windows to be sealed, so they could not escape. He intended to keep them there until they starved.

Days went by, and they had nothing to eat or drink. Finally, Rat said, "This is a job for me," and he began gnawing through the wood. Then, he went to various houses and took meat, rice, and other food.

After a few days, when Kanu's men saw that they were still alive, they brought brush to set fire to the house. Anteater said, "Here is a job for me." Anteater began to dig. Faster and faster he dug, until finally he dug a hole right under the wall. The four friends escaped.

Kanu Above said to himself, "These creatures are very clever! But I will trick them." He said to them, "I will return the child if you can pick her out from all the other children here."

Fly buzzed into the dressing room and noticed one girl who received no help from the others. She had to braid her own hair and put on her own beads, bracelets, and ankle jewelry. Fly flew back to his friends and said, "The girls will all be dressed alike, but watch which one jumps. That is our chief's daughter."

Fly buzzed over all the girls and, spotting the one he knew to be the "outsider," he bit her. Whoop! She immediately jumped. The four friends grabbed her and said, "This is the one. We choose her!"

Kanu Above was impressed, "You are very clever, indeed. Take the girl, and here are four kola nuts for her father, to show my admiration for the four of you."

So the four friends climbed back down with the chief's daughter and presented the happy girl to her father . . . along with the four kola nuts.

"See this," Kanu Below said to his people. "You wanted to banish these four from our village, but it is they who have returned my daughter to me. I am so grateful to them that I have decided they will be my under chiefs from now on."

And it was so.

Telling Tips

This story, unlike many European stories, features groups of four rather than three. There are four under chiefs, four animals, four pesky attributes, four ways that Kanu Above tries to get rid of them, four ways they trick Kanu, and even four kola nuts. Like Native American stories, African stories often rely on the number four. An easy way to remember the sequence is to visualize each scene and keep the four animals in the order they are introduced with their pesky attribute: 1. Spider, web; 2. Rat, gnawing and stealing food; 3. Anteater, digging holes; and 4. Fly, biting. Each pesky attribute is also the thing that serves them well while trying to save the daughter: Spider weaves a web to the sky so they can find the daughter; Fly sees that the meat is poisoned and they do not eat it; Rat gnaws and finds food when they are starving; Anteater digs a hole in the floor so they can escape; Fly bites the girl so that they can identify her.

This story lends itself to opportunities to use body language to convey traits of the characters. When each of the pesky animals is brought before Kanu Below, use your body to convey the mood. Stand tall, lean forward, and speak toward the floor as though someone very tiny stands before you. When each animal replies to Kanu Below, look up to exaggerate the difference in size and power.

Try making your voice smaller for the small creatures. Because there are many characters in this story, do not try to give each a unique voice. It becomes too difficult to keep the voices straight. When the creatures approach Kanu Above, you might want to continue looking up when they speak, but stand with a firm stance and a bit stronger voice to show that they are determined to stand up to Kanu Above.

Story Path

1. Introduce Kanu Above and Kanu Below and the problem: Kanu Above came and took Kanu Below's daughter.

2. The four under chiefs come and complain about four animals followed by an explanation from the animal.

    a. Spider spins webs that people run into. He does it to catch food.

    b. Rat gnaws holes and steals food. He takes only enough.

    c. Anteater digs holes in the ground and villagers fall. He is searching for ants.

    d. Fly buzzes around and bites villagers. He bites only when people swat at him.

3. Each time the chief sees good and gives another chance, and the teller says, "And it was so."

4. The second part of the story has the four animals agreeing to find and bring back his daughter.

5. Spider spins a web to the sky.

6. Kanu Above is not happy about this but tries to get rid of them four times.

    a. He poisons the food but Fly warns his friends.

    b. He seals the house to starve them but Rat gnaws a hole and steals food.

    c. He tries to burn them out but Anteater digs a tunnel.

    d. He challenges them to find the real daughter and Fly bites her so she jumps.

7. Kanu Above is impressed and realizes that they have special powers, so he gives them the girl and four kola nuts.

8. Kanu Below makes them his under chiefs for their bravery and for being such good citizens.

Right There

1. What were the names of the two great chiefs in this story?

2. Why was Kanu Below sad?

Think and Search

1. When we first meet the creatures (Spider, Rat, Anteater, and Fly) what does each of them do that makes them appear to be bad citizens?

2. What special skill does each creature use when meeting Kanu Above?

Author and Me

1. Do you think that Rat, Anteater, Spider, and Fly had an obligation to help Kanu Below?

2. Who was a more powerful leader, Kanu Above or Kanu Below? Why?

3. Which leader was more fair? Why?

4. Each creature used his special skill to help Kanu Below. As citizens of a community, what special skills can you use to help others?

5. What lesson about citizenship do you think the teller wanted us to learn from this tale?

On My Own

What does this quote from Andrew Jackson mean to you? "The brave man inattentive to his duty is worth little more to his country than the coward who deserts in the hour of danger."

Post-Telling

Return to the Walk and Gawk chart papers to add new ideas.

Additional Sources

Books

Abrahams, Roger D. *African-American Folktales: Stories from Black Traditions in the New World.* New York: Random House, 1999.
    This collection of tales gathered by Joel Chandler Harris, Zora Neale Hurston, and Roger Abrahams and others will provide the reader or teller with creation stories, moral fables, and plantation journals.

Web Sites

This Web site provides access to a wide range of civics lesson plans: http://www.teach-nology. com/teachers/lesson_plans/history/civics.

Fairness

Pre-Telling—On My Own

1. Have you ever watched any of the shows featuring court cases and judges on TV?

2. Do you ever try to guess what the judge will say after listening to both sides of the argument?

3. Think of some decisions you have had to make: which outfit to purchase, which extracurricular activity to join, which present to purchase for someone. What other decisions have you had to make? Why can it sometimes be so difficult to make a final decision?

Walk and Gawk

Assign students to one of the charts that has a question about Fairness. Students brainstorm ideas as an On My Own activity and return to it after the discussion as an Author and Me activity.

Setting up the Story

Have you ever heard of the English monarch called Queen Elizabeth? (Explain that Queen Elizabeth of the twentieth and twenty-first centuries is a descendant of Queen Elizabeth I.) Have you ever heard of a ruler from India named Akbar the Great? (Most students probably have not because our history classes usually highlight Western European countries, not Eastern dynasties.) This story will give both sides of an argument over a mango tree. See if you can figure out who is the rightful owner before the end of the story.

Predict-A-Character: Make a prediction about characters you will be meeting in the story. Match the character traits or descriptions to the characters.

Characters:

- Akbar, ruler of India

- Charan, a young farmer

- Birbal, a poor man

- Yusuf, an old farmer

Character Traits or Descriptions:

a judge	a true friend	a brilliant man
unscrupulous	honest	fair
resourceful	sentimental	generous

"Akbar and Birbal—the Mango Tree,"
a tale from India as told by Megan Hicks

Background Information: Akbar ("the Great") ruled the Mughal Empire of India (1556–1605) at the same time that Queen Elizabeth I ruled the British Empire (1558–1603). Both rulers are considered among the greatest monarchs the world has ever seen.

Akbar's closest friend, Birbal, was also his most capable and honest judge. Birbal was a brilliant man, but he came from a poor family, and he was self-educated. Because his family was poor, and Hindu at that, the other lawyers and judges in Akbar's court despised Birbal. They, like Akbar, were descended from royal Muslim families and had attended all the best schools.

This is a story of how Akbar believed that his most humble subjects deserved the same attention and justice that the nobility felt entitled to.

One day when court was in session, two farmers, Charan and Yusuf, came to Akbar and other judges with a dispute about a mango tree.

Charan, young and strong, stood tall and with a loud voice said, "I come in search of truth and justice. A mango tree grows on the border between my farm and the farm of my neighbor, Yusuf.

Yusuf keeps chasing me off whenever I try to gather up a few mangoes for my family. He claims all the fruit is his, but I'm the one who waters the tree and takes care of it."

Akbar turned to Yusuf and asked, "How do you respond to that statement?"

Yusuf hobbled forward. He was old and bent, and his voice cracked.

"I planted that tree on the morning my first son was born," he said. "Through the years that tree has blessed my family with shade, with fruit, and with a place for songbirds to perch. I'm happy to share with my neighbor, but Charan picks the tree bare and sells the fruit in the market and leaves none for me."

Akbar turned to the judges present. He asked, "And what is the judges' verdict?"

Sitting in their seats of authority, the judges snickered among themselves and rolled their eyes.

One of them said, "It's one man's word against the other. The tree grows on the border between two farms. No one can tell for certain who owns this tree. The judges have concluded that these two fools should be whipped and fined for wasting the court's time with this frivolous case." They nudged each other with their elbows and laughed. All of them, that is, except Birbal.

Akbar said, "Birbal, you seem to have a different opinion. Have you arrived at a different verdict?"

"I have arrived at no verdict," Birbal answered. "I ask that court be adjourned until this time to-morrow."

The other judges shook their heads and whispered, "He is stymied by a case this inconsequential! What does Akbar see in him?"

Akbar, however, nodded soberly and said, "Very well. Court is adjourned until tomorrow."

That night, Birbal covered himself in a hooded cape and went to the house of Charan. He banged on the door with a heavy stick.

"Wake up, Charan! Wake up!" he cried. "Thieves are stealing your mangoes! Wake up!"

For a long time there was no answer. But finally Charan's voice called out, "Let a man sleep, will you? Do you think I'm going to trouble myself over a few wormy mangoes? Go away."

Birbal nodded to himself and went across the fields to the house of Yusuf. Pounding on the door, he called out, "Yusuf! Yusuf! Thieves are stealing your mangoes!"

Instantly, Birbal heard Yusuf's voice from inside the house. "Wife! Wife! Help me find my stick. Where are my robe and sandals? If it isn't enough that Charan wants to cheat me, now I must guard the tree from vandals."

From the shadows Birbal watched. Even though Yusuf saw no vandals, he climbed up into the branches of the tree and settled in to spend the night guarding it.

Next morning both men returned to court; Charan looking rested, Yusuf looking haggard from a long night of no sleep.

Akbar said, "Well, Birbal, are you closer to a verdict today than you were yesterday?"

"I am not," Birbal confessed. "I could not determine beyond doubt who is the rightful owner of the tree."

The other judges grinned, shook their heads, and whispered to each other, "We told Akbar that yesterday."

Birbal continued, "So here is what I propose. I propose that all the mangoes be picked and divided equally between the two farmers, that the tree then be cut down and chopped into firewood and that the firewood, too, be divided equally between them."

Now the other judges thought to themselves, "Why didn't we come up with a clever solution like that?"

Akbar asked Charan and Yusuf, "Do each of you find this arrangement to your liking?"

Charan grinned triumphantly and, bowing low, said, "The decision is just and fair and wise. I will happily abide by these terms."

But Yusuf said nothing. Akbar turned to him and asked, "Yusuf, are you not pleased with the terms of the verdict?"

Yusuf approached Akbar and said, "Majesty, that tree has become to me as dear as a member of my family. If anything should happen to it, I would feel as though one of my children had died. I will give up any claim to the tree and let it go to Charan. But please, please, do not harm it."

Silence fell over the court, for now the truth of the matter had become evident to everyone in the room. Everyone now knew that Yusuf had always been the rightful owner of the mango tree.

Akbar looked at Yusuf and said, "The tree is rightly yours and shall belong to you and your family for as long as it lives."

To Charan he said, "You, Charan, I give you a choice: Thirty lashes with a whip, or a fine of thirty pieces of silver to punish you for wasting the court's time with your false claims."

Charan chose to pay the thirty silver pieces, which Akbar then handed over to Yusuf.

"Once again," he announced, "Birbal is the one who has seen into the heart of the matter so that justice may be served."

About the Teller

Storyteller Megan Hicks graduated from the University of Oklahoma School of Library and Information Studies and served for many years as a children's librarian for the Central Rappahannock Regional Library system in Virginia. Author, performer, and producer of two award-winning storytelling recordings, she travels throughout the United States and internationally, sharing stories with audiences of all ages and all walks of life. Visit her Web site at http://www.meganhicks.com or send her an e-mail at megan@meganhicks.com.

Telling Tips

This story needs more setup time because there are numerous characters involved. It requires strong listening skills so students can keep the names and characters straight.

In addition, this story has two stories running through it. First, the wise decision of who owned the mango tree and, second, the understory of Judge Birbal, who was despised by the other judges. This provides two avenues for discussions on honesty (fairness over the mango tree) and caring (being fair to others by accepting them for their talents, not for their choice of religious practices or lack of education). In telling this story, it may be interesting to stop at two points in the story and ask some questions: After Charan and Yusuf give their arguments before the judge, ask the class if they can predict who is the rightful owner. Then, after they return to court and Birbal shares his decision to divide the mangoes equally and cut the tree down, ask the class, if they think that is a good decision, why or why not?

The teller can also use some subtle body language to help listeners infer the character traits of the two farmers. Facial expressions and gestures can help students to infer the character traits of each man.

Story Path

1. Introduction about the time and place of the story, as well as the characters' names—Akbar, Birbal, Charon, and Yusuf.

2. Charon comes to court and declares that his neighbor, Yusuf, is stealing his mangoes.

3. Yusuf says the mangoes are his and that Charon has been taking them and selling them, leaving his family with no mangoes.

4. The judges say there is no way to judge it, because it is one man's word against another. They want them both flogged.

5. Akbar asks Birbal his opinion; Birbal wants a recess so he can find out who is the true owner.

6. That night Birbal disguises himself and goes to Charon's house saying that vandals are destroying the tree. Charon tells him he doesn't care.

7. Birbal then goes to Yusuf's home and tells him of the vandals; he protects the tree all night.

8. The next day, when the judges ask Birbal who owns the tree, he feigns ignorance but offers a viable solution: split everything from the tree—mangoes and the wood after they chop it down.

9. Charon readily agrees, but Yusuf is horrified at the prospect of losing the tree, so he gives up any claim to it.

10. The judges and court understand that Yusuf is the true owner.

11. Akbar gives Charon a choice: thirty lashes or thirty pieces of silver for wasting the court's time.

12. Birbal once again proves to be a wise judge.

Right There

1. What were the names of the two people who went to court?

2. What were their occupations?

3. What were they disputing?

Think and Search

1. Name three reasons that the other judges disapproved of Birbal.

2. Relate the sequence of events that occurred on the evening that Birbal disguised himself and called out a warning of vandals to Charan and Yusuf.

Author and Me

1. Compare the testimony of the two farmers. How does each testimony reveal the characteristics of each man?

2. Did the storyteller do anything to help the listeners to infer character traits? (Provide students with the following passage from the story. Let them work with a partner to retell the passage; encourage them to use body language to convey each man's character.)

    Charan, young and strong, stood tall and with a loud voice said, "I come in search of truth and justice. A mango tree grows on the border between my farm and the farm of my neighbor, Yusuf. Yusuf keeps chasing me off whenever I try to gather up a few mangoes for my family. He claims all the fruit is his, but I'm the one who waters the tree and takes care of it."

Yusuf hobbled forward. He was old and bent, and his voice cracked. "I planted that tree on the morning my first son was born," he said. "Through the years that tree has blessed my family with shade, with fruit, and with a place for songbirds to perch. I'm happy to share with my neighbor, but Charan picks the tree bare and sells the fruit in the market and leaves none for me."

3. At the end of the story Charon had to choose a beating or a fine, and he chose the fine. Was it fair that Akbar gave the coins to Yusuf? Why or why not?

4. Does this story remind you of any other story you may have heard about fairness?

Post-Telling

- Return to the Walk and Gawk chart papers to add new ideas.

- Return to the Predict-A-Character and align the character traits and descriptions.

Compare and Contrast

Compare the courtroom as you perceive it in the United States to the courtroom as portrayed in the story. (In the United States, there is a head judge in charge of proceedings, but also 12 other "judges," which together are called a *jury*. The jury is made up of citizens from the community. They work on one case and make the decision of guilt or innocence. In India, the judges are all learned men who give their opinions on all the cases presented in the court, and the main judge makes the decision. What are the pros and cons of each system?

Additional Sources

Books

Sarin, Amita. *Akbar and Birbal.* New York: Penguin, 2005.

This is a collection of tales that have passed from generation to generation. It is filled with historical information on the Mughal Empire. The stories present a range of characters dealing with ethical and personal dilemmas.

Web Sites

Read the online story "Truth Always Finds Its Way" and compare the two stories (both have Akbar, Birbal, and a mango tree; both have a problem that seemingly cannot be resolved; both have Birbal finding out the truth in a clever way; both have an "underdog" as the truthful person; etc): http://www.geocities.com/shishusansar/birbal/birbal46.htm.

Honesty

Pre-Telling—On My Own

1. Why do you think some people like to gossip?

2. What are the most common topics for gossip?

3. Is there a difference between gossip and dishonesty?

4. Is there a difference between telling the truth and telling the whole truth?

5. Can gossip ever be used for a good purpose?

Walk and Gawk

Assign students to one of the charts that has a question about honesty. Students brainstorm ideas as an On My Own activity and return to it after the discussion as an Author and Me activity.

"Gettle's Wagging Tongue," a traditional Jewish tale as told by Diann Joy Bank

Once there lived a young girl named Gettle who lived in a small village. She had fun making up stories full of unkind words about neighbors and classmates. She would skip up and down the brick streets with her light brown braids flying up in the air. Everyone would say, "Gettle is such a gossip! She is always making up stories that are not true. Her tongue wags all day and all night!"

The apple seller cried, "Because of that little girl's wagging tongue, no one wants to buy my beautiful apples. They are picked fresh from my own apple trees. Gettle tells everyone that I put rotten apples in the bottom of their paper bags that I sell to them. I would never do such a thing!"

The baker shouted, "That Gettle is ruining my business. I do not put burned bagels at the bottom of my customers' bags. I am an honest man."

Gettle didn't understand why no one liked her. "I'm just having fun!" She and her parents were never invited to anyone's home. Gettle was never asked to any birthday parties. "Why don't I have any friends?" she asked her parents.

"It's because of your nasty wagging tongue telling all those stories about our neighbors," her parents said sadly. The villagers all complained to the rabbi and asked him to stop Gettle's wagging tongue.

The rabbi immediately went to Gettle's house. "Rabbi, we need your help with Gettle," her parents said with a sinking heart. "She never listens to us! She thinks it's funny to make up stories about everyone."

"Bring her to me right now. I'll wait outside your home," the rabbi said.

Bursting through the door, Gettle saw the rabbi. "Do you want to hear more of my silly stories?" Gettle giggled. "My stories are only words. I can take them back whenever I want. I like the story I made up about Sara having a Pinocchio nose and Jacob always walking on his tiptoes. I laugh a lot at my story about you, rabbi. Have you heard? The rabbi gets lost wherever he goes," she giggled.

The wise rabbi told Gettle to bring her feather pillow to him. In a blink of an eye, she ran to her bed and brought her pillow to him. He took a small pair of scissors out of his pants pocket and began to cut open one end of the pillowcase. "Listen closely, Gettle. Would you like to play a game? Go to

Main Street in the center of the village and toss the feathers to the wind. Then come back to me," smiled the rabbi.

She did exactly what the rabbi asked as she danced round and round waving her pillowcase up in the air. The feathers spun up and around as they were carried in the wind. She returned to the rabbi. "I love that game, Rabbi," she said with glee.

"Good," said the rabbi, as he pulled a new pillowcase from his pants pocket. "Now, I want you to take this pillowcase and gather up all the feathers that you released and bring them back to me," said the rabbi.

Gettle was so excited to play the rabbi's game. She ran up and down the streets, jumping and leaping into the air, trying to catch the floating feathers. The feathers were up in the trees and flying out of her reach.

Soon, she returned to the rabbi crying, "It's impossible to gather up all those feathers. The wind carried them away from me."

"Gettle!" the rabbi said wisely, "your words are just like those feathers. You don't know where your words travel. They go in and out of many ears that listen. You don't know what harm they can do to others."

Gettle cried. "Now I understand! I can't take my words back. No one will ever like me again! I'll never have friends. My stories were not funny at all. They hurt everyone in our village," Gettle sobbed. "I don't like my wagging tongue of stories anymore! I'm so sorry, Rabbi, but no one will ever listen to me again!"

The rabbi smiled, "You can do a *mitzvah*. It's never too late to be kind. You must go to each person you told an unkind story about. Tell them you are sorry from your heart and ask for forgiveness! Tell them you will change your ways."

So, she did. Eventually, Gettle became known as the village storyteller, remembering to only tell stories that made everyone feel happy.

About the Teller

Diann Joy Bank, professional storyteller and educator, employs audience participation in her storytelling performances and workshops. In her published works, *Grandma Annie's Gourmet Delights* and "The Negune Tune" in the book *First Harvest, Jewish Writing in St. Louis,* she evokes our imaginations to teach values from her multicultural and Jewish folklore centered on character development themes. With her experience as a teacher in early childhood, an ESL teacher, and an assistant teacher in elementary schools, Diann would be delighted to share her stories with you. Contact her at dbanktells@sbcglobal.net or visit her Web site: http://www.diannjoybank.net.

Telling Tips

This is a traditional tale that can be told in a straightforward and easy manner. It follows a logical sequence, has few characters, and is easy to follow.

Story Path

1. Introduction to Gettle who likes to gossip; townspeople voice their complaints.

2. Apple seller and baker lament that Gettle has ruined their business with her gossip.

3. Gettle cries to parents that no one likes her.

4. Rabbi visits the home at parents' request.

5. Gettle tells the rabbi some of her gossip.

6. The rabbi asks her to play a game and release the feathers from her pillow on Main Street.

7. Gettle returns, and the rabbi asks her to collect the feathers.

8. Gettle attempts to collect the feathers but returns to say that it is an impossible task.

9. Rabbi makes the comparison between gossip and the feathers.

10. Gettle understands and repents.

Right There

1. When you first meet Gettle, what is her favorite thing to do?

2. Who comes to talk with Gettle?

Think and Search

1. What types of things were people throughout the community saying about Gettle?

2. Who were some of the people Gettle had gossiped about?

Author and Me

1. Gettle's gossip hurt sales for some of the businesspeople in her community. If people knew that Gettle was a gossip, why do you think they believed her lies about the apple seller and the baker?

2. Is Gettle gossiping or being dishonest? Is there a difference?

3. The story ends with Gettle becoming the village storyteller, telling only happy stories. Do you think people will ever really trust Gettle again?

4. The villagers approached the rabbi to solve their problem with Gettle. What else could they have done to solve this problem?

On My Own

1. How would days at our school be different if no one gossiped?

2. Is there a difference between telling the truth and telling the whole truth?

Post-Telling

Return to the chart papers to add new ideas.

Additional Sources

Books

Forest, Heather. *Wisdom Tales from around the World*. Atlanta, GA: August House, 1996.
  A retelling of folktales, proverbs, and parables that reflect a range of cultural and religious roots. Each tale has explanatory notes that provide insight. These stories are not just for primary students. Forest's tellings provide plenty of material for discussion.

Fox, Paula, and Erika Meltzer. *One-Eyed Cat*. New York: Simon & Schuster Children's Publishing. 2000.
  Temptation becomes too much for Ned Wallis. Even though he is forbidden to touch the rifle, he sneaks it out of the house. He takes one shot in the dark and now must deal with his guilt.

Rothenberg, Joan. *Yettele's Feathers*. New York: Hyperion Books for Children, 1996.
  In this adaptation, the gossip is an older woman without children who spends a great deal of time minding other people's business. She spreads rumors, has facts wrong, and presumes the worst about everyone.

Web Sites

This Web site offers different versions of this story: http://www.story-lovers.com/listsgossipstories.html.

Respect

Pre-Telling—On My Own

  1. How does treating people with respect affect your opinions of them?

  2. Is respect from others something that we must earn?

  3. Are there certain individuals who should always be treated with respect?

Walk and Gawk

Assign students to one of the charts that has a question about Respect. Students brainstorm ideas as an On My Own activity and return to it after the discussion.

"The Wooden Bowl," a Japanese tale as told by Wendy Gourley

In Japan, a young bride moved into her husband's house. The new husband and wife were good and kind to each other and all would have been well, except the husband's father who lived with them. The father was old and feeble. His hands shook, and he did not see very well. He often spilled his food or dropped things. The husband was often impatient with his father.

"Why should I have to take care of the old man?" said the husband. "When I was growing up, he hardly had a kind word for me! He never paid me any attention! Why should I be burdened with him now?"

One night at dinner, the old man dropped his bowl of rice, shattering the china bowl into many pieces and scattering rice in all directions.

"Look what you have done now!" bellowed the young husband. "Do you think I have money to replace all the things that you have broken? This is the final straw! You will have to sit in the corner from now on and eat from this wooden bowl."

The husband picked up a simple wooden serving bowl and tossed it into the corner.

The old man bowed his head. His daughter-in-law helped him to the corner and got him more food in the wooden bowl. The rest of the meal passed in silence.

Although the woman loved her husband, she was ashamed of the way that he treated his father. She believed that no matter what the past troubles had been between them, a father as an elder is deserving of kindness and caring. And so she came up with a plan.

Before evening the next day, she came to the old father and told him to break the wooden bowl at dinner.

"Oh, no! I cannot do that! My son will be very angry if that happens!" cried the old man.

"Please trust me," said the kind daughter-in-law. "All will be well."

So it was, that night at dinner, the old man dropped his bowl, breaking it in two.

The old man cowered, unsure of what was going to happen. The husband scowled and was about to open his mouth to speak, when his wife jumped to the side of the old man. She picked up the pieces of the bowl and shook them at the old man and scolded, "What have you done, old man?! This is very bad. Do you not know that I was saving this bowl for my own husband when he grows weak and feeble?"

The young man hung his head in silence and thought. Then, without saying a word, he got up and gently led his father back to the table. He dished up some food in a china bowl and placed it before his father. From that time forward, the old father was treated with honor and respect.

About the Teller

Wendy Gourley is a professional storyteller, writer, and playwright. She is the managing director of Resonance Story Theatre. Visit her Web site at http://www.wendygourley.com.

Telling Tips

This is a simple straightforward tale to tell. Once you have learned the story path, feel free to add details to meet the needs of your audience.

Story Path

1. The young man is impatient with his aged father, who spills a great deal of food.

2. He voices complaints that his father had no time for him as a child.

3. When the father drops and breaks his china bowl, the son forces him to sit in the corner and eat from a wooden bowl.

4. The young wife helps her father-in-law and then comes up with a plan.

5. She instructs the old man to break his wooden bowl and assures him it will be all right.

6. The old man breaks the wooden bowl.

7. Before the son can say anything, the young wife laments that she had hoped to save that bowl for her own husband to use in his old age.

8. The son, realizing his disrespect, brings his father back to the table.

Right There

1. Why is the old man eating from a wooden bowl?

2. Who devises the plan to shame the son?

Think and Search

1. Sequence the plot of the story.

2. List the actions of the son and list the actions of the young wife.

Author and Me

1. Do you think that the son was justified in treating his father so poorly?

2. When you look at the actions of the son, do you think his behavior is controlled by his emotions or his character traits?

3. When you look at the actions of the wife, do you think her behavior is controlled by her emotions or character traits?

On My Own

1. Are there certain individuals who should always be treated with respect?

2. Do you think your treatment of people today will affect the way they treat you at another time?

3. Is respect a noun or a verb?

4. Is the respect of others something that must be earned?

Post-Telling

1. Return to the chart papers to add new ideas.

2. Make a list of people who might try your patience or people you might have difficulty tolerating—for example, a rude store clerk, someone who has an annoying habit, someone with poor hygiene.

3. What are some strategies or techniques you can use to make sure you always treat others with respect?

Additional Sources

Books

Paulsen, Gary. *The Monument.* New York: Random House Children's Books, 1993.

This is the story of a young girl named Rocky who, at the age of nine, is adopted by a kind but alcoholic couple. When an artist named Mick comes to Kansas to create a monument for their heroes of war, Rocky's life changes. The artist, at times dirty, vulgar, and hard-drinking, is dedicated to his art. In three short days, Mick quiets the town gossips and reveals the power of art.

Web Sites

This Web site offers lesson plans on respect: http://www.educationworld.com/a_lesson/lesson/lesson329.shtml

The first seven minutes of this video is a retelling of "The Wooden Bowl." The final two minutes is a plea to help stop elder abuse: http://www.youtube.com/watch?v=-TC1w3qKQec

Responsibility

Pre-Telling—On My Own

1. What personal responsibilities do you currently have in your life?

2. Are there ever times that it is difficult to live up to your responsibilities?

3. What might make it difficult to live up to responsibilities?

4. What happens if you shirk your responsibilities?

Walk and Gawk

Assign students to one of the charts that has a question about Responsibility. Students brainstorm ideas as an On My Own activity and return to it after the discussion as an Author and Me activity.

"James Cash Penney," researched and written by Carol Watkins

James Cash Penney was one of twelve children. His father was a part-time preacher and farmer living near Hamilton, Missouri. James's father tried to teach his children to be hardworking and responsible. By the time James was eight, he was milking cows twice a day and helping his father plow, plant, and harvest crops on the farm. The family had plenty of food, but they had little money for things like clothing and shoes. One day, James's father told him that, now that he was eight going on nine years old, he would be responsible for buying his own clothes and shoes. James looked down at his one pair of shoes. Each had a large hole in the sole.

"Please, Dad, won't you buy me one more pair? Both of these shoes are worn out," James pleaded.

"I'm sorry, son," his father said. "You will have to begin now to provide these things for yourself."

That night, when James went to bed, he thought and thought. He had saved $2.50 from running errands and doing chores for neighbors. But that was not enough to buy shoes and clothes for a whole year. He remembered that his father often bought a calf and kept the calf until it was grown and sold it for more than he had paid for it. He didn't have enough to buy a calf, so he bought a pig for $2.50 and built a pen for it using some scrap wood.

He studied how his father had built a feeding trough for his animals. Then James built his pig a feeding trough just like the one his dad had made. He had a trough, but had no money left to buy food for his pig. He remembered that his mother saved table scraps to feed their pig. So James went to several neighbors and asked them if he could collect their garbage pails every day. He told them he would return their pails shiny and clean each evening. The neighbors were happy to have James take their garbage pails and have them returned clean. James fed his pig the garbage. The pig grew and grew until it was big enough to sell.

James got a good price for his pig, enough to buy two more. He fattened them up and sold them. In time, he had eleven pigs. He found more neighbors to collect garbage from and gathered corn left behind by the harvesters who had picked the corn on neighboring farms. One day, James's father told him that he would have to sell all of his pigs. "But they aren't fully grown yet, Dad," James explained. "I'll only get half of what I would get if I sold them when they are bigger."

"The neighbors are complaining about the smell, James," Mr. Penney said. "You must sell the pigs tomorrow." The next day James sold his pigs for exactly half of what they would have sold for if he could have waited until they were fully grown.

"What did you learn from selling the pigs?" his father asked.

"I learned that I lost half of what I could have made if I had not sold them before they were ready," James replied.

"No," said his father. "The lesson you should have learned is consideration of others. When you had a few pigs it was fine; but when you tried to raise so many pigs, the smell became so strong that our neighbors complained. You were trying to make a lot of money; but you were not considering the effect it was having on others. Live by the Golden Rule, Son: treat others how you want to be treated."

For his next money-making adventure, James bought some seed and planted watermelons. The melons ripened just in time for the county fair. He parked his father's wagon, filled with watermelons just outside the entrance to the fairgrounds. "Here they are, folks! Sweet watermelons! Watermelons! Get your watermelons here! Big ones for ten cents, good ones for five cents!" Soon, James was selling watermelons as fast as he could hand them out of the wagon.

His selling was interrupted by his father who ordered him to return home. James obeyed his father, but he was angry. Once they arrived home, his father explained, "All the other people selling things at the fair had to pay a fee in order to sell their wares on the fairgrounds. This fee goes to support the fair. You parked outside of the fairgrounds and did not pay a fee. By not paying anything toward the support of the fair, you had an advantage over those who did. You were competing unfairly. Remember the Golden Rule, Son. Treat others the way you want to be treated."

When James grew up, he never forgot the lessons he had learned as a boy. As an adult, James worked several years as a clerk in a general store. After he developed health problems, he moved to Denver, Colorado. There, he bought a butcher shop. Because he refused to be bribed by the chef of a big hotel, who bought lots of meat from James, the chef bought his meat from someone else, and James's butcher shop failed.

James then bought an interest in a chain clothing store in Wyoming. The stores were named The Golden Rule. James liked the name "The Golden Rule." The Golden Rule means to treat others the way you would like to be treated. This was a part of his upbringing.

In time, James bought into two other Golden Rule stores. After a few years, he bought out his two partners and became the owner of a small chain of three stores. From this beginning, the small chain of stores grew into the world's largest dry goods store chain. In time, the name was changed from Golden Rule to the name of its founder, J. C. Penney. James always kept the lessons he learned as a boy as the fundamental policies for operating his stores. He shared his profits with those who served him faithfully over the years.

About the Teller

Carol Watkins has a B.S. in elementary education and more than twenty years teaching experience. For twelve years, she worked as an educational consultant and curriculum writer. She has been working as a professional storyteller for seven years. Send her an e-mail at cwatkins@mail.win.org or visit her Web site: http://www.storytellercarolwatkins.com.

Telling Tips

This is an historical story. To tell it, you need to be true to the facts, but you don't need to adhere to the way the teller presented them—use your own words and sentence patterns. The storyteller did a lot of research to write this story. Whenever telling an historical tale, it is wise to read another biography to confirm the facts. There is a lot more to J. C. Penney's life, but the storyteller carefully crafted the story to keep only those details that supported her theme of responsibility.

Of course, the teller did not know exactly what was said between the father and the son; that part is fictionalized to keep the story interesting. Dialogue keeps your listeners listening. So, although you need to know the facts and not alter them, in your retelling, you can use your own words in the dialogue. Besides, it makes it easier to remember a story when you say it in your words.

The structure of the story is like most biographies—early years in Missouri, struggling entrepreneur, successful businessman. Using that structure will help you remember the story. Keeping the identity of "J. C. Penney" a secret until the end of the story will give the audience an "aha" moment, a very satisfactory way to end a story.

Story Path

1. James Cash Penney was born into a poor family in southern Missouri.

2. As a child, he was greatly influenced by his father, a Baptist minister, who instilled in him the value of responsibility (working to pay for his own clothes) and of following the Golden Rule (consideration for neighbors while trying to raise pigs and paying for fees so as not to take advantage of other vendors).

3. He moves to Denver, Colorado, where he tries various occupations.

4. He fails as a butcher because of his integrity in not giving in to the unscrupulous chef.

5. J. C. moves to Wyoming, where he buys into the Golden Rule store.

6. Through his penchant for keeping to the values of the Golden Rule that his father taught, he was able to increase sales and become successful.

7. Later the stores were called JC Penney after their owner.

Right There

1. At what age was James made responsible for purchasing his own shoes?

2. How many brothers and sisters did James have?

3. How did he manage to gather enough food to feed his pigs?

4. Why did he have to sell his pigs before they were fattened?

Think and Search

1. What two things did James Cash Penney's father stop him from doing?

2. What lesson did the father reinforce to his son both times that he stopped him?

Author and Me

1. Do you think James Cash Penney's father was proud of him?

2. Do you think that James Cash Penney learned the lessons his father wanted him to learn?

3. Did James Cash Penney demonstrate a responsible attitude toward his family? Toward his community? Toward the world?

4. To help him manage his dry good stores, James Cash Penney developed some ideas that he called the "Penney Principles." How do these principles apply or not apply to your life?

James Cash Penney called the following lessons the "Penney Principles":

1. To serve the public, as nearly as we can, to its complete satisfaction.

2. To offer the best possible dollar's worth of quality and value.

3. To strive constantly for a high level of intelligent and helpful service.

4. To charge a fair profit for what we offer and not what the traffic will bear.

5. To apply this test to everything we do: "Does it square with what is right and just?"

On My Own

Why do you think some people feel they have no responsibilities to their community or to the world?

Post-Telling

- Return to the chart papers to add new ideas.

- Look at the list of responsibilities you made before hearing the story of James Cash Penney. Now think about what it means to be a responsible person and complete the following chart.

What Responsibilities Do You Have in Each of the Following Areas of Your Life?	
Responsibilities to My School and Community	Responsibilities to the World

Poetry

Create an *I Am* poem as J. C. Penney, his father, one of his employees, or one of his neighbors.

Additional Sources

Books

Bartone, Elisa. *Pepe the Lamplighter*. New York: Scholastic; Lothrop, Lee & Shepherd Books, 1993.

In the 1800s Pepe's father brought his large family to America from Italy. Pepe felt a responsibility to help support the family. Unfortunately, Pepe's father disapproved of his son's job. Pepe shows great strength of character throughout the story.

Hudson, Wilma J. *J. C. Penney: Golden Rule Boy*. New York: Atheneum, 1972.

A biography about James Cash Penney, whose knack for earning a dollar combined with the lessons learned from his father led to the establishment of a nationwide chain of dry goods stores.

Lasky, Kathryn. *She's Wearing a Dead Bird on Her Head*. New York: Hyperion Books for Children, 1999.

This is the true story of two women who were shocked with the destruction of song birds for high fashion. They took it upon themselves to do the work necessary to establish the Audobon Society in Massachusetts at the turn of the century and stop the slaughter of song birds.

Stanley, Jerry. *Children of the Dust Bowl: The True Story of the School at Weedpatch Camp.* New York: Crown Books for Young Readers, 1993.

    This is the story about Leo Hart, who made it his responsibility to create a federal emergency school for children who lived at Weedpatch Camp, a farm-labor camp built by the federal government during the Dust Bowl years.

Web Sites

Visit a site called "Being Responsible Builds Character": http://www.school-for-champions.com/character/responsible.htm

Works Cited

Blachowicz, C. L. Z. Making Connections: Alternatives to the vocabulary notebook. *Journal of Reading* 29(7): 643–649.

Ideas Plus: Book 4. Urbana, IL: National Council of Teachers of English. 1986.

Ideas Plus: Book 20. Urbana, IL: National Council of Teachers of English, 2002.

Johns, Jerry L., and S. D. Lenski. *Improving Reading: A Handbook of Strategies.* Dubuque, IA: Kendall Hunt, 1997.

National Council of Teachers of English. *A Position Statement from the Committee on Storytelling.* 1992. Available at http://www.ncte.org/positions/statements/teachingstorytelling.

National Council of Teachers of English & International Reading Association. *Standards for the English Language Arts.* 1996. Available at http://www.ncte.org/standards.

Raphael, Taffy E., & Au, Katherine. QAR: Enhancing Comprehension and Test Taking across Grades and Content Areas. *The Reading Teacher* 59(3): 206–221.

Raphael, Taffy E., K. Highfield, and K. H. Au. *QAR Now: A Powerful and Practical Framework That Develops Comprehension and Higher-Level Thinking in All Students.* New York: Scholastic, 2006.

Sprenger, Marilee. *How to Teach So Students Remember.* Alexandria, VA: Association for Supervision and Curriculum Development, 2005.

United States Department of Labor. *The Secretary's Commission on Achieving Necessary Skills.* Washington, DC: Government Printing Office, 1991.

Vygotsky, L. S. *Mind in Society.* Cambridge, MA: Harvard University Press, 1978.

Walsh, John. *The Art of Storytelling: Easy Steps to Presenting an Unforgettable Story.* Chicago, IL: Moody, 2003.

Wilhelm, Jeffrey. *Action Strategies for Deepening Comprehension.* New York: Scholastic Professional Books, 2002.

Wormelli, Rick. *Metaphors & Analogies: Power Tools for Teaching Any Subject.* Portland, ME: Stenhouse, 2009.

Yopp, Hallie Kay, and Ruth Helen Yopp. *Literature-Based Reading Activities,* 4th ed. New York: Pearson, 2006.

Web Sites with Featured Quotes from the Text

http://www.quotationspage.com

http://www.brainyquote.com

http://www.alberteinsteinsite.com/quotes/einsteinquotes.html

Index

About the Authors

PHYLLIS HOSTMEYER has been telling stories all her life but never realized she was a storyteller until she joined the Riverwind Storytellers. Thanks to the encouragement and support of Marilyn Kinsella and the members of Riverwind, Phyllis now enjoys many opportunities to entertain with fairy tales and fables that she transforms into rap and rock. But the true power of story comes alive for her when she regales people with tales of her family and growing up in a small Southern Illinois community where she still lives. One moment she touches your heart with her personal stories of healing then she lifts your spirit with laughter. For the chance to bond with listeners, Phyllis will travel anywhere. Local libraries; the Great Hall of the People in Beijing, China; classrooms; libraries; and national conferences have all been a part of her venue. Not only a storyteller, but also an educator, Phyllis offers workshops on storytelling in the classroom and demonstrates how this art enhances reading and writing skills. Working as a consultant for Educational Resources Groups, Inc., of Charleston, South Carolina, Phyllis also conducts professional development sessions on literacy strategies and presents research-based methods for teaching reading and writing. In the past three years, she has conducted more than 200 workshops throughout the United States and Canada.

Her personal Bundle of Sticks includes her friends, her years as a classroom teacher, her work as an educational consultant, and her life as a storyteller. Her family, Rebecca and John, Eva, Kayla, and Jordan, provide Phyllis and her husband Bob with a wealth of stories. She dedicates this book to her family whose love and support have taught her about the importance of unity.

Since 1981, MARILYN ADELE KINSELLA of Fairview Heights, Illinois, has called herself "Taleypo the Storyteller." As a Southern Illinois University elementary education graduate and teacher, she began telling stories in her classroom and applying those stories to her curriculum. She now gives workshops to teachers on the use of storytelling in the classroom and to tellers on how to develop useful study guides for school visits. The most popular Web pages on her Web site include those under "Teacher/Teller."

After teaching for eleven years, she began work as the storyteller at the Edwardsville Public Library where she honed her more than two hundred stories to include all age groups. She gives workshops to librarians on ways to use storytelling and story extensions during the library story times. Currently she is a full-time teller of tales and travels extensively around the Midwest and beyond telling stories and doing workshops. She has been a featured teller at many festivals including the Illinois Storytelling Festival and the St. Louis Storytelling Festival. Yearly, she travels to many schools and libraries throughout the Midwest.

Her stories and articles have appeared in many books and magazines including *The Storytelling Classroom: Applications across the Curriculum, The Big Book of St. Louis Nostalgia,* and *Guidepost's Christmas Miracles.*

As coartistic director of the Belleville Festival of Stories, she works with BASIC Initiative to develop unique ways to provide character education to students through the festival, summer camp workshops, and study guides on her Web site. Her collaboration with her coauthor, Phyllis Hostmeyer, has opened new ways of presenting stories that not only entertain but provide sound academic questions and activities to enhance the telling experience.

Her personal Bundle of Sticks includes her educational background, her public library work, her stories, and her involvement in storytelling. These sticks are lovingly wrapped together with the strong ties of love from her family: Chrissie, Amy, Brian, Drew, and, most of all, her husband Larry. She dedicates this *Bundle of Sticks* to the memory of her mother, whose stories inspired her story to come to life.